Season of Breakthrough, Healing & Restoration

Dr. Cassundra White-Elliott

DR. CASSUNDRA WHITE-ELLIOTT

Season of Breakthrough, Healing & Restoration

"And after you have suffered a little while, the God of all grace, who has called you to his eternal glory in Christ, will himself restore, confirm, strengthen, and establish you."
1 Peter 5:10 (ESV)

Season of Breakthrough, Healing & Restoration
by Dr. Cassundra White-Elliott

Copyright © 2025 by Dr. Cassundra White-Elliott.
Cover copyright © 2025 by CLF Publishing Collaborative, LLC.
Cover design by Senir Design. Contact info: info@senirdesign.com.

CLF Publishing Collaborative, LLC supports the right to free expression and the value of copyright. The purpose of copyright is to encourage writers and artists to produce the creative works that enrich our culture.

The scanning, uploading, and distribution of this book without express permission is a theft of the author's intellectual property. All rights reserved. No portion of this book may be reproduced, stored in a retrieval system, or transmitted by any form or any means electronically, photocopied, recorded, or any other except for brief quotations in printed reviews, without the prior permission of the publisher. If you would like permission to use material from the book (other than for educational or review purposes), please contact clfpublishing.org via the Contact Us link. Thank you for your support of the author's rights.

CLF Publishing Collaborative, LLC
Hesperia, CA 92345
Visit us at clfpublishing.org

First Edition: August 2025

Library of Congress Cataloging-in-Publication Data
Names, White-Elliott, Dr. Cassundra, author.
Title: *Season of Breakthrough, Healing & Restoration*
Description: First Edition. | Hesperia, California: CLF Publishing Collaborative, LLC, 2025. | Includes biblical references. Audience: Ages 13 and up. | Summary: Inside, *Season of Breakthrough, Healing, and Restoration*, you will find biblical wisdom, honest prayers, and powerful testimonies that will stir your faith and remind you that God is still in the business of turning things around. Whether you are in need of healing, desperate for breakthrough, or longing to feel whole again, know you are not alone - and your season is about to shift. Let this be your guide as you step into everything God has prepared for you.

Identifiers: LCCN 2025912791 | ISBN 9798992578423 (paperback)

ISBN 979-8-9925784-2-3 (paperback)

CONTENTS

Introduction: Getting Started ... 7

Chapter One: Cultivating a Spiritual Breakthrough ... 9
   Biblical Breakthrough Examples ... 12
   Modern-Day Breakthrough Examples ... 20
   Cultivating Your Breakthrough ... 24
   Benefits of a Spiritual Breakthrough ... 29
   Receiving a Breakthrough ... 32
   My Breakthrough (poem) ... 39
   Note Pages ... 40

Chapter Two: Walking in Your Healing ... 45
   Biblical Examples of Healing ... 49
   Modern-Day Healing Examples ... 62
   Do You Require Healing? ... 71
   The Healing Process ... 82
   Signs of Emotional Healing ... 84
   A Journey to Healing (poem) ... 89
   Note Pages ... 90

Chapter Three: Activating the Power of Restoration ... 95
   Restoration Via a Biblical Lens ... 98
   God Restores in Multiple Areas ... 101

Biblical Examples of Restoration	103
Modern-Day Restoration Examples	119
Why Restoration is Necessary	128
The Process of Restoration	131
How to Receive Restoration	135
Living in the Fullness of Restoration	138
He Restores (poem)	143
Note Pages	144
Conclusion: Stepping into the New	149
Additional Books by the Author	151
About the Author	153

Introduction: Getting Started

Season of Breakthrough, Healing, & Restoration is designed to guide you through one of the most powerful transformative journeys of your life. Whether you are facing personal challenges, emotional wounds, or spiritual struggles, this book is a beacon of hope, reminding you that no matter how dire the situation may seem, there is always the promise of breakthrough, healing, and restoration, when you place yourself and the situation into God's hands.

This book expresses that life's trials are not to be ignored but acknowledged as opportunities for growth, renewal, and divine intervention. It is a call to enter a season where your dreams, your health, your relationships, and your spirit can experience the powerful touch of God's grace (unmerited favor) and tender mercies. It will empower you with faith to press forward into your breakthrough, the wisdom to embrace healing, and the understanding to receive restoration in every area/season of your life.

Through each chapter, you will be guided to embrace a mindset of victory, even in the midst of your struggles. You will learn practical tools and biblical principles (by reading biblical and modern-day testimonials and verses) that will inspire you to walk confidently into your breakthrough. As you turn each page, prepare to unlock divine healing (for your mind, body, and spirit) and prepare for the restoration of what was lost or broken.

This is your season - a season of transformation, renewal, and lasting peace. The path forward may not be easy to navigate, but with unwavering faith and the lessons found within these pages, you will discover the best is yet to come. Haggai 2:9 states, *"The glory of this latter house shall be greater than of the former, saith the LORD of hosts: and in this place will I give peace, saith the LORD of hosts."* During the time this passage was written, "the house" referred to the temple in Jerusalem. Today though, the "house" can refer to your body as the temple of Holy Spirit, comparing your former state/condition with your new state, the one that will manifest after your breakthrough, healing, and restoration. Further-more, Job 8:7 says, *"Though thy beginning was small, yet thy latter end should greatly increase."* What God has designated for you is expressly for you. So, take hold of it!

Chapter One

Cultivating a Spiritual Breakthrough

Chapter One
Cultivating a Spiritual Breakthrough

Everyone will experience at least one tragedy in life, whether it is physical, emotional, psychological, educational, financial, sexual, or familial. These tragedies may be life altering or simply mind boggling, throwing the person for an unexpected loop, possibly sending him/her onto a different trajectory than the one he/she started upon. What determines whether a tragedy will be less scarring or potentially debilitating is how the person responds amidst the crisis but more importantly afterward. If the individual is able to extract purpose from the suffering and is then able to progress in life rather than becoming stagnant, reverting to negative behaviors, or engaging in detrimental activities, the person can be said to have experienced a "breakthrough."

Let's explore the term "breakthrough" and more specifically "spiritual breakthrough." While the term "spiritual breakthrough" is ubiquitous in a variety of spiritual arenas, it is not a term found in the Holy Bible or in any other universally employed resources, such as dictionaries or encyclopedias. Therefore, any derived definition is subjective to the individual. With that in mind, I define "spiritual breakthrough" as a unique experience that refers to a significant moment of personal growth, or it may be a realization one has on a spiritual level, or it may be a combination of both. Alternately, the experience may be the resolution of an ongoing issue or struggle in the person's life or a deeper understanding of one's relationship with God.

Whatever the case, the experience can be equated to an epiphany, which is an experience of a sudden and striking realization (awareness) or insight (deep understanding). This does not mean a physical, spiritual, or positional change in one's life will occur instantaneously simply because the awareness was sudden. There is work to be done for the breakthrough to be fully realized.

Furthermore, the experience will be unique for each person and usually offers profound peace, emotional healing, and/or clarity. Therefore, it is not important or necessary to align your experience with someone else's to determine whether or not you are having or have had a breakthrough. If you feel a change is on the horizon, take hold of it, and experience all life has for you. Trust the Lord to order your steps as you navigate through your "breakthrough," and embrace the life that comes after it.

Biblical Breakthrough Examples

From the Old Testament to the New Testament of the Holy Bible, there are a variety of examples of individuals who experienced a spiritual breakthrough. We are able to read example after example of individuals breaking free from their past lives, being delivered from strongholds, having revelations, being enlightened by God's Word, etc.

In the New Testament, the Book of Acts, also known as the Acts of the Apostles, is filled with accounts of individuals experiencing breakthroughs. These examples give us hope that there are opportunities of freedom and spiritual newness for each of us, untethering us from situations that attempt to keep us bound and not walking in God's will for our lives. Included in the next section are three such examples.

Acts Chapter 9 shares the account of Saul of Tarsus traveling on the Damascus Road. The following summary provides the key points of his breakthrough.

The Damascus Road Experience: Saul, a zealous Pharisee and a fierce opponent of the early Christian movement, believed Christians were blasphemers. He actively persecuted Christians, even overseeing the stoning of Stephen, who was the first martyred Christian (Acts 7:58), and hunted them down to imprison them. His mission to arrest more Christians led him to travel to Damascus, while possessing a letter of authorization from the high priest.

Saul's Breakthrough
Acts 9:1-20

As Saul approached Damascus, suddenly a bright light shone about him, and he fell to the ground. He heard a voice saying, *"Saul, Saul, why are you persecuting me?"* Confused, Saul asked, *"Who are you, Lord?"* The voice responded, *"I am Jesus, whom you are persecuting. Now get up and go into the city, and you will be told what you must do"* (Acts 9:4-6). The light faded, and Saul was left blind. His companions led him into the city, where he remained blind for three days, as he fasted and prayed.

During that time, Saul's world was drastically turned asunder. He realized the very person he was persecuting, Jesus, is the true Messiah. That revelation allowed Saul to break free from his former life and prepare to walk in a new calling, one that would offer individuals life rather than ushering them into a life filled with pain and fear at Saul's hands as a result of their belief and faith in Jesus.

In Damascus, a Christian named Ananias, acted on God's instruction, went to Saul, restored his sight, and baptized him. Saul's breakthrough was complete as he was filled with the

Holy Spirit, his sight was restored, and he was immediately baptized into the faith he once sought to destroy.

Saul later became an apostle of the Lord (taking his newly given name Paul) and eventually wrote thirteen books of the New Testament of the Holy Bible, known as the Pauline epistles. Paul was the second author after Luke (who penned the Book of Luke and the Book of Acts) to pen a large portion of the New Testament. Paul's "spiritual breakthrough" was a pivotal moment in Christian history, which led to him becoming one of the most influential figures in spreading the Gospel.

> **Joshua 24:15**
> *"And if it seem evil unto you to serve the Lord, choose you this day whom ye will serve; whether the gods which your fathers served that were on the other side of the flood, or the gods of the Amorites, in whose land ye dwell: but as for me and my house, we will serve the Lord."*

Ponder this: When Saul was blinded by the light and subsequently fell to the ground, he literally had a choice to make as we all do when a dichotomy is placed before us. Saul was comfortable in the life he had been living.

As a Jew who studied under Gamaliel, a leading authority in the Sanhedrin, Saul was very proud of his Jewish roots, training, and knowledge of Jewish law. Anyone who opposed Judaism, by turning away from its religious practices and becoming followers of the Way, found themselves enemies of Saul.

However, when the Lord Jesus addressed Saul on the Damascus Road, essentially halting him in his tracks, telling him he had been persecuting Him, Saul had to make an instant decision: Would he ignore the voice of the Lord and continue on his way, or would he give an ear to the Lord and bring his present activities of persecuting Christian believers to an end? Obviously, Saul chose the latter, and his life (along with the lives of countless others) was changed.

God has a plan for each one us. In His unique design for mankind, He afforded us free will, allowing us to make personal decisions, including the choice of who we will serve (Joshua 24:15). We can choose to serve false gods or God Almighty, the one who created the heavens and the earth. Although God gave us free will, His desire is for all mankind to serve and worship Him. Saul's personal choice led to a path of newness, one that afforded him an opportunity to have a relationship with the risen Savior, Jesus the Christ. Just imagine how Saul's life would have been different, along with the lives of many others, if he would have continued on his predetermined plight. Thank God for His intervention.

In the next chapter of the Book of Acts, a spiritual breakthrough is shown to have taken place in Peter's life. Read the summary of the account. In Acts Chapter 10, Peter experienced a significant spiritual breakthrough that challenged his understanding of God's mission and the scope of the Gospel. The event unfolded in two key parts:

1. *Vision of the Sheet* (Acts 10:9-16): While praying on a rooftop in Joppa, Peter had a vision of a large sheet descending from heaven, filled with all kinds of animals, both clean and unclean, according to Jewish law. A voice instructed Peter to "kill and eat," but Peter initially refused, saying he had never eaten anything impure. The voice replied, "Do not call anything impure that God has made clean." The vision occurred three

Peter's Breakthrough
Acts 10:9-48

times, teaching Peter that God's grace extends beyond traditional Jewish dietary laws *and* includes all people.
2. *Peter's Encounter with Cornelius* (Acts 10:17-48): Soon after the vision, Peter was invited to the house of Cornelius, a Roman centurion, who had also received a divine message. Cornelius, a Gentile, had been seeking God, and Peter realized God's message of salvation is not limited to Jews but is also for Gentiles. Peter preached the Gospel to Cornelius and his household, and the Holy Spirit came upon them, confirming that Gentiles are now included in God's plan of salvation. That encounter marked a key moment in the early church's expansion, when Peter acknowledged that God does not engage in partiality.

The breakthrough shifted Peter's understanding, demonstrating the Gospel is for all people, regardless of ethnicity or background, and it initiated the broader inclusion of Gentiles into the Christian community. Notice how Peter's vision was the catalyst for his spiritual breakthrough, which in turn prepared him for the following encounter he experienced at the home of Cornelius.

Ponder this: Like Saul, Peter had been taught to operate within the strict guidelines of Judaic laws and customs. Although he had converted to Christianity, his entire life *before* he walked with Christ and *as* he walked with Christ was in alignment with the Torah, as Jesus Himself was a practicing Jew. For Peter to shift his mindset from what he had always known and lived by proved to be quite challenging for him just as it would for anyone who has held a practice or custom for any length of time. When a new method is introduced, it may take time to adapt, especially if there is resistance.

When Peter first had the vision of the sheet, which was filled with both clean and unclean animals, his initial response was, "No," as he had predisposed specifications about his eating practices. But God, who initially showed Peter the vision, brought the vision to Peter twice more. Finally, Peter understood the revelation and shifted his mindset, which was his breakthrough.

The shift permitted the next phase to occur, which was the full opening of the sheep gate, allowing Gentiles to freely receive Christ as their personal Lord and Savior. If Peter had not received what the Lord had presented before him, he could not have effectively served as an apostle to both the Jews and Gentiles. When God desires us to break away from one activity or mindset to another, He can be quite persistent. Ultimately though, the decision to receive the enlightenment and make the necessary change is ours.

Because Peter allowed the Lord to teach him a new principle, he was able to be effective in preaching the Gospel to Jews, offering them an opportunity to convert from Judaism to Christianity and be forgiven of their sins and also to Gentiles, providing them the same opportunity of being forgiven of their sins by a Savior who died for all mankind.

In Acts Chapter 16, we are provided with yet another example of a spiritual breakthrough. This time it occurred in the life of Lydia. Lydia experienced a spiritual breakthrough during Paul's missionary journey to Philippi. The key points of her breakthrough are as follows:

1. *Lydia's Encounter with Paul* (Acts 16:11-14): Paul and his companions, including Silas, arrived in Philippi, where they found a group of women gathered for prayer by the river. Lydia, a wealthy merchant who dealt in

> **Lydia's Breakthrough**
> Acts 16:11-15

purple cloth, was among them. She is described as a "worshiper of God," meaning she was a Gentile who believed in the God of Israel. As Paul spoke to the group, Lydia's heart was opened by the Lord, and she responded to Paul's message about Jesus.

2. *Lydia's Baptism and Hospitality* (Acts 16:15): After accepting the Gospel, Lydia and her household were baptized, marking a significant moment of spiritual transformation. She then urged Paul and his companions to stay at her home, offering them hospitality as an expression of her new faith and commitment to the Christian community.

Lydia's spiritual breakthrough was realized because she first had a willingness to receive Christ as her personal savior as she had been yearning for Him. When Paul came and preached the Gospel to her and her family, the seeds had already been planted, and Paul was there to water them. Then, God gave Lydia "the increase" (1 Corinthians 3:6-7) in Him, receiving her into His family as an adopted daughter (Ephesians 1:4-5; Galatians 4:5; Romans 8:15; John 1:12). That was the breakthrough she desired and subsequently received.

Ponder this: Often times, people do not want to engage in practices with individuals who are different than they are for fear they may be rejected from the dominant group. However, Lydia did not allow fear of the unknown to grip her heart. She had obviously heard about God and allowed Him to stir a longing desire within her for Him. Then, the opportunity for her to enter in a direct relationship with God was presented, and she did not falter or take time to second guess the situation.

Many times, we miss our opportunity for breakthrough because we second guess ourselves and even God, causing us to become stagnant, thereby keeping change and progress at bay. Like Lydia, we must be proactive in our own lives, seizing opportunities when they arise, trusting God has our best interest in mind.

When we have an intense desire for something (i.e. freedom, deliverance, peace, renewed joy, etc.), we begin to lay the foundation in preparation for what is to come, even when we do not know what is on the horizon. This is applicable in all the scenarios you just read, even the one of Saul of Tarsus, who was diametrically opposed to the new Way. Saul had a deep love and reverence for God, and upon his encounter with the Lord Jesus, the love Saul already possessed for God allowed the Son of God to enter into Saul's life and have full control. Saul did not know he needed a breakthrough, for he believed he was correct in his actions of harming Christians. However, when the opportunity suddenly presented itself in Saul's life, he readily accepted what God had for Him.

Look at the result it made in Saul's life and in the lives of believers worldwide, as they read the epistles and other books of the Bible he authored as Apostle Paul, a servant of the Lord Jesus the Christ. Having a spiritual breakthrough can be life changing, and while it obviously impacts the life of the person who experiences it, it may also impact the lives of those with whom the person comes in contact. Who knows, maybe your breakthrough will impact others with whom you come in contact.

Modern-Day Breakthrough Examples

Spiritual breakthroughs are not something that is exclusive to those who lived in biblical times. As God is no respecter of persons, He is still manifesting spiritual breakthroughs in our time. In this section, modern-day examples of breakthroughs will be shared to further exemplify how a breakthrough can occur and send the individual on a different, healthier, positive, and more hopeful trajectory in life.

Tiffany's Breakthrough in Forgiveness

For years, Tiffany struggled with deep resentment toward her father for abandoning the family when she was a child. Even as an adult, she carried the pain of abandonment and as a result, built walls around her heart, refusing to forgive him. Despite being a devoted member of her church, she felt disconnected from God, unable to reconcile her faith with her anger and hurt.

One evening, Tiffany decided to attend a church retreat focused on forgiveness, hoping something would break or shift inside her. She knew she could not continue functioning the way she had been. During a meditation session, she was invited to reflect on any grudges or hurts she was holding onto. As she closed her eyes, she remembered a moment from her childhood when she longed for her father's love and attention. In that memory, she saw herself sitting in the living room, waiting for him to return, but he never did. As the image flooded her mind, she felt a surge of sadness and anger.

However, in that moment, Tiffany sensed a still, small voice within her urging her to let go. She visualized herself standing face-to-face with her father, not as a child filled with bitterness, but as an adult who had found peace within. She felt a wave of compassion toward him, realizing his abandonment was not a reflection of her worth, but of his own brokenness.

Tears flowed, but they were tears of release, not anger. Tiffany began to forgive him in her heart. The breakthrough was not immediate or easy, but as she continued to process her emotions, she found a deeper connection to God and a sense of liberation she had not felt in years. The burden of unforgiveness began to lift, and Tiffany felt more at peace, knowing true healing would come when she chose forgiveness, just as she had been forgiven by God.

James' Breakthrough in Purpose

James is a successful lawyer in his mid-thirties, but for years, he felt an underlying dissatisfaction with his career. He followed the traditional path laid out for him - prestigious education, job promotions, and financial success - but he felt empty and disconnected from a deeper sense of purpose. He spent long hours at work, but every evening, he felt exhausted and unfulfilled. His relationships were strained, and he started questioning if there was more to life than his career.

One day, James attended a seminar on personal growth, not expecting much but hoping for a distraction from his daily routine. The speaker talked about living a life aligned with one's core values and passion, emphasizing true success is not about external achievement but about internal fulfillment. The speaker shared a story of a person who left his corporate job to become a social worker, helping children in need. The story resonated deeply with James, sparking something inside him he had not acknowledged before. He had always been

> **James'
> Breakthrough**
> Internal Fulfillment

passionate about mentoring and advocating for underprivileged youth, but he had buried that passion under the pressure to achieve material success.

That night, James went home and reflected on his life, asking himself what truly brings him joy and fulfillment. He started to connect the dots. His deep dissatisfaction stemmed from the fact that his work did not align with his values. After much reflection, he decided to begin volunteering at a local youth center during his weekends. His small steps into the new realm ignited something in him. He felt more energized, more alive, and more connected to his true self.

His breakthrough was not about quitting his job immediately, but rather about aligning his work and personal life with his deeper purpose. Over time, James gradually transitioned into a career that allowed him to combine his legal skills with his passion for social justice, finding a meaningful way to serve others and, in the process, rediscovering his own sense of purpose.

Teresa's Breakthrough in Self-Acceptance

Teresa is a young woman in her twenties who has always struggled with body image issues. Growing up, she was constantly compared to her more conventionally attractive peers, leading her to develop a deep sense of insecurity. Despite her achievements - graduating with honors, securing a job she loves, she had always felt her appearance held her back from truly being accepted by others. She obsessed over diets, exercise routines, and social media comparisons, but nothing seemed to change her perception of herself.

Teresa's Breakthrough
Body Image

One day, Teresa's therapist suggested a body positivity workshop. At first, Teresa was skeptical, thinking it was just another superficial attempt to love yourself without doing the real work. But she decided to go, mainly out of curiosity. During the workshop, the facilitator invited the group to stand in front of a mirror, look at themselves, and list things they love about their bodies, without focusing on appearance but rather on functionality and health.

When it was Teresa's turn, she hesitated but eventually started engaging by listing her strong legs that carry her through long walks, her hands that help her write, and her heart that loves deeply. For the first time in her life, Teresa looked at herself in the mirror without judgment, recognizing the value of her body beyond societal standards.

Later, as the facilitator spoke about how everyone's body is unique and worthy of respect, Teresa realized the years she spent criticizing herself were rooted in comparison and external validation. She finally realized self-acceptance does not mean conforming to an ideal but embracing her own individuality and value. The breakthrough came when Teresa shifted from trying to fit into a mold to accepting her body as it is - flaws and all.

She began to practice self-compassion, starting with small acts like eating nourishing foods, practicing yoga for wellness rather than weight loss, and celebrating what her body allows her to do. Over time, Teresa's sense of self-worth shifted from outward appearance to an inner sense of acceptance and gratitude for her body. She found freedom in no longer needing to compare herself to anyone else, and for the first time, she felt truly at peace in her own skin.

Cultivating Your Breakthrough

Achieving a spiritual breakthrough typically requires intentional steps that involve both inner reflection and outward action. While the path to spiritual growth is unique for each person, here are some common steps that can guide someone toward experiencing a spiritual breakthrough:

1. *Acknowledge the Need for Change*
    - Reflection: The first step is acknowledging that something needs to shift in your life. This could be a sense of emptiness, disconnection, confusion, or a longing for deeper meaning. Acknowledging the need for spiritual transformation or growth is the beginning of any breakthrough.

> **Romans 12:2**
> *"And be not conformed to this world: but be ye transformed by the renewing of your mind..."*

    - Openness: Be open to the idea that God may want to teach you something new, help you heal, or lead you in a new direction.

2. *Create Space for Quiet and Solitude*
    - Time for Prayer/Meditation: Set aside time for quiet reflection, prayer, or meditation. This space allows you to listen for God's voice and become more aware of any spiritual stirrings within. It is often in stillness that breakthroughs occur.
    - Silence the Noise: In a busy world full of distractions, it is important to create moments of solitude where you can disconnect from the hustle and bustle, and truly focus on your spiritual needs.

> **Psalm 1:2**
> *"But his delight is in the law of the Lord; and in his law doth he meditate day and night."*

3. *Surrender and Let Go of Control*
   - Humility: Acknowledge that you cannot achieve a break-through on your own. Surrender your desires, plans, and anxieties to God, recognizing you need divine guidance and help.

   > **I Peter 5:6-7**
   > *"Humble yourselves therefore under the mighty hand of God, that he may exalt you in due time: Casting all your care upon him; for he careth for you."*

   - Letting Go: Sometimes, breakthroughs happen when we let go of our preconceived notions, pride, or unhealthy attachments. Release the things that hold you back from fully embracing spiritual growth.

4. *Seek Guidance Through Scripture or Biblical Teachings*

   > **II Timothy 2:15**
   > *"Study to shew thyself approved unto God, a workman that needeth not to be ashamed, rightly dividing the word of truth."*

   - Study the Holy Bible: As a believer, immersing yourself in the scriptures can reveal new insights, wisdom, and perspectives that trigger a breakthrough.
   - Spiritual Mentorship: Seek counsel from spiritual leaders, mentors, or counselors who can provide

guidance and wisdom in times of spiritual struggle or confusion.

5. *Embrace Prayer (Communication with God)*
    - Honest Communication: Engage in prayer (or any form of direct communication with God) with honesty, openness, and vulnerability. Share your struggles, doubts, and desires. Prayer can be a powerful tool for transformation.

    > **Luke 18:1**
    > *"And he spake a parable unto them to this end, that men ought always to pray, and not to faint."*

    - Listening: Just as important as speaking in prayer is the act of listening. Pay attention to any answers, insights, or peace that arises in your spirit.

6. *Repentance and Forgiveness*
    - Repentance: A spiritual breakthrough often requires letting go of past mistakes, sin, or guilt. Repenting

    > **Matthew 6:14-15**
    > *"For if ye forgive men their trespasses, your heavenly Father will also forgive you: But if ye forgive not men their trespasses, neither will your Father forgive your trespasses."*

    means acknowledging areas where you have gone astray and seeking forgiveness. This is a release of burdens that can allow spiritual renewal.
    - Forgiving Others: Forgiving those who have wronged you is crucial for a breakthrough. Holding onto grudges

can block your spiritual growth. Letting go of resentment creates space for healing and transformation.

7. Act on Insights or Inspiration

- Obeying Promptings: When you sense a shift or hear a message, whether through prayer, scripture, or inner conviction, act on it. Spiritual breakthroughs are often about putting faith into action - whether it is a change in behavior, mindset, or relationships.

> **James 2:17**
> *"Even so faith, if it hath not works, is dead, being alone."*

- Making Changes: This might involve altering unhealthy habits, reconciling with people, or stepping into new areas of service or ministry.

8. Be Patient and Trust the Process

- Trust in Timing: Oftentimes, a breakthrough take time. Trust that the process is unfolding even when immediate results are not visible. Spiritual growth often comes in layers, and breakthroughs can take time to fully manifest.

> **James 1:4**
> *"But let patience have her perfect work, that ye may be perfect and entire, wanting nothing."*

- Faith: Maintain faith, even when things feel stagnant. Believe the breakthrough is on the horizon, and trust God is working in ways you might not immediately understand.

9. *Celebrate and Cultivate Gratitude*
    - Recognize the Breakthrough: When you experience the shift, whether big or small, take time to celebrate and recognize the spiritual growth. This reinforces the importance of the breakthrough and helps you remain aware of the transformation.
    - Gratitude: Cultivate a heart of gratitude for the lessons, the challenges, and the moments of clarity. Thankfulness can deepen your connection to God and help sustain the breakthrough.

> Psalm 118:1
> *"O give thanks unto the Lord; for he is good: because his mercy endureth for ever."*

10. *Stay Committed to Ongoing Growth*
    - Continuous Reflection: Spiritual breakthroughs are not a one-time event but part of an ongoing journey. Continue to seek growth, understanding, and intimacy with God. Regular practices of prayer, reflection, and community will help you stay rooted in your spiritual path.

> Ephesians 4:14 *"That we henceforth be no more children, tossed to and fro, and carried about with every wind of doctrine..."*

   - Engage with Community: Surround yourself with a supportive spiritual community that encourages and holds you accountable as you continue to grow in your faith.

Key Note: A spiritual breakthrough is not always an instantaneous or dramatic event. Rather, it is a gradual transformation that can result in lasting change. The key is openness, patience, and the willingness to surrender to a greater plan than your own.

Benefits of a Spiritual Breakthrough

Recall the earlier provided examples of biblical and modern-day individuals who experienced a breakthrough. After each person's breakthrough, they all went on to live a life with Christ that was vastly improved from the life they were previously living due to the unique breakthrough experience. (And, that does not mean their lives were substandard prior to the breakthrough. It only means God took them to another level in Him and with Him.) The improved life was a direct result of gaining a number of benefits from the list below and perhaps other benefits which are not listed. Be aware that all individuals may not obtain the exact same benefits. Also, there is a chance that an overlap of benefits may occur between two individuals.

1. *Renewed Connection with God*

A spiritual breakthrough often leads to a stronger and more intimate relationship with God. It may involve a deeper experience of God's love, presence, and peace. This can be the result of prayer, worship, Bible study, or even quiet reflection. For many, a breakthrough is characterized by a profound sense of God's nearness and an increased awareness of His will, which often-times may be in contradiction to the person's will. For this reason alone, a spiritual breakthrough often leads to spiritual growth and development.

2. Overcoming Sin and Temptation

One of the most common breakthroughs is the victory over habitual sin or temptation. The breakthrough could be a moment when someone is freed from an addiction, a destructtive habit, or a deep emotional wound. This type of breakthrough often involves repentance, a turning away from sin, and a renewed commitment to live according to God's statutes, with the power of Holy Spirit enabling this transformation.

When this particular gain is realized in someone's life, it is best to not resist the leading of Holy Spirit, for He is far more equipped to attend to the necessary details of the transformation. Remember the Word of the Lord in Zechariah 4:6, *"Then he answered and spake unto me, saying, This is the word of the L*ORD *unto Zerubbabel, saying, Not by might, nor by power, but by my spirit, saith the L*ORD *of hosts."*

3. Understanding and Receiving God's Grace

Spiritual breakthroughs often lead to a deeper understanding and appreciation of God's grace. For we are informed, *"My grace is sufficient for thee: for my strength is made perfect in weakness. Most gladly therefore will I rather glory in my infirmities, that the power of Christ may rest upon me"* (II Corinthians 12:9).

As believers grow in their faith, they may have a breakthrough whereby they come to *fully* realize they are saved by grace alone and not by their works (Ephesians 2:8-9). This can be liberating, as they let go of striving or trying to earn God's approval and instead rest in the sufficiency of Christ's sacrifice on Calvary's cross. For, Hebrews 10:10 states, *"By the which will we are sanctified through the offering of the body of Jesus Christ once for all."*

4. Increased Faith and Trust

A spiritual breakthrough may occur when individuals move from doubt or fear into greater trust and faith in God's plan for their life. Matthew 21:21 empowers us: *"Jesus answered and said unto them, Verily I say unto you, If ye have faith, and doubt not, ye shall not only do this which is done to the fig tree, but also if ye shall say unto this mountain, Be thou removed, and be thou cast into the sea; it shall be done."* This can be in the form of trusting God's promises, even when circumstances are difficult. It could be a time when the individuals move from merely knowing about God to truly trusting Him with their future, finances, relationships, health, and all other decisions.

5. Empowerment through Holy Spirit

Holy Spirit plays a crucial role in spiritual break-throughs. Through Holy Spirit, believers can experience empowerment for living a victorious Christian life. This may involve the gifts of the Spirit, such as wisdom, knowledge, faith, healing, miracles, prophecy, discerning of spirits, different kinds of tongues, and interpretation of tongues. I Corinthians 12:8-10 states: *"For to one is given by the Spirit the word of wisdom; to another the word of knowledge by the same Spirit; To another faith by the same Spirit; to another the gifts of healing by the same Spirit; To another the working of miracles; to another prophecy; to another discerning of spirits; to another divers kinds of tongues; to another the interpretation of tongues."* A spiritual breakthrough often comes with the realization that we do not have to rely on our own strength but can live empowered by Holy Spirit to overcome challenges and live victoriously. Many times, it is this truth that catapults believers into their breakthrough.

6. Biblical Transformation

A breakthrough may also involve a new level of understanding of Scripture and how it applies to life. When a person begins to grasp biblical truths more deeply or applies them in practical ways, it can lead to personal transformation. This transformation often shifts one's perspective on issues like relationships, finances, work, and priorities, all aligned with God's Word.

7. Inner Healing

Emotional and mental healing is another powerful aspect of spiritual breakthroughs, for *"He heals the brokenhearted and binds up their wounds"* (Psalm 147:3). Many believers experience breakthroughs when they are healed from past hurts, trauma, or unforgiveness. Through the power of prayer, counseling, and support from the Christian community, individuals can experience restoration and peace in areas where they have been broken or wounded.

8. Purpose and Calling

A spiritual breakthrough can also help us clarify or discover our divine purpose. Some believers experience moments where they discern their calling more clearly, whether it is to serve in ministry, in their community, or in a particular area of work. This clarity can bring a new sense of direction and fulfillment, as the individuals align more closely with God's mission for their life.

Receiving a Breakthrough

There are moments in life when we come to the end of ourselves, when our strength is exhausted, our resources are depleted, and nothing we try seems to move the mountain in front of us. It is in these moments that we are primed for a breakthrough. In this section, we will explore what it means to position our hearts to receive breakthrough, through faith, surrender, persistence, and the supernatural power of God. Your breakthrough may be closer than you think.

1. *How to Embrace the Change that Comes with Breakthrough*

Breakthroughs in life often come with significant change. Whether it is a breakthrough in one's personal, professional, spiritual, or relational life, change is inevitable. Learning how to embrace change is key to fully experiencing and sustaining the benefits of the breakthrough.

- *Acknowledge that Change is Part of God's Plan:* Change may feel uncomfortable at first, but it is important to remember God has a purpose in every shift. Breakthroughs often push us out of our comfort zones and require us to adapt to new circumstances. The Bible teaches us that God has plans to prosper us, even through changes: *"For I know the thoughts that I think toward you, saith the LORD, thoughts of peace, and not of evil, to give you an expected end"* (Jeremiah 29:11).
- *Trust in God's Timing and Sovereignty:* When breakthrough comes, we often struggle with impatience or doubt, but trusting in God's timing can ease the anxiety that comes with change. He makes all things beautiful in His time. *"He hath made every thing beautiful in his time: also he hath set the world in their heart, so that no man can find out the work that God maketh from the beginning to the end"* (Ecclesiastes 3:11).
- *Release Fear and Step Into Faith:* Breakthroughs often require stepping into the unknown. When faced with new challenges, it is easy to fear failure or uncertainty.

Embracing the breakthrough means choosing faith over fear. *"For God hath not given us the spirit of fear; but of power, and of love, and of a sound mind"* (II Timothy 1:7).

Example:

When the Israelites crossed the Red Sea, they experienced a monumental breakthrough that led to freedom. However, they also had to embrace the change of living in the wilderness (as opposed to living in Egypt) before reaching the Promised Land. This required trust in God and a willingness to embrace the unfamiliar. The trust that was required was not acquired overnight. The Israelites often complained to Moses saying, *"Is not this the word that we did tell thee in Egypt, saying, Let us alone, that we may serve the Egyptians? For it had been better for us to serve the Egyptians, than that we should die in the wilderness"* (Exodus 14:12). After some time, their faith increased, and they placed their trust in the Lord.

2. Maintaining a Spirit of Gratitude and Celebration

A crucial aspect of receiving one's breakthrough is maintaining a spirit of gratitude and celebration. Breakthrough is a gift, and cultivating an attitude of thankfulness ensures we honor God for what He has done. Gratitude keeps us grounded and helps us focus on the blessings rather than any struggles we may encounter in the process.

- *A Heart of Thanksgiving is Key to Receiving More Blessings:* Recognizing the significance of a breakthrough with a thankful heart is a way of acknowledging God's goodness. The Bible says, *"In every thing give thanks: for this is the will of God in Christ Jesus concerning you"* (I Thessalonians 5:18). Thankfulness

does not mean ignoring challenges but appre-ciating God's hand in bringing us through them.
- *Celebrate God's Faithfulness:* Celebrating a breakthrough involves more than just acknowledging one's success. It is about recognizing God's faithfulness and goodness. Through celebration, we testify to others of God's faithfulness. The psalmist says, *"I will bless the Lord at all times; his praise shall continually be in my mouth"* (Psalm 34:1, ESV).
- *Testify of Your Breakthrough:* Sharing testimonies is a powerful way of celebrating God's goodness. It encourages others and strengthens our own faith. *"And they overcame him [Satan] by the blood of the Lamb, and by the word of their testimony; and they loved not their lives unto the death"* (Revelation 12:11).

Example:
King David's life was filled with both trials and breakthroughs, yet throughout it all, he continually praised God. When the Ark of the Covenant was returned to Jerusalem, David danced and celebrated, saying, *"It was before the LORD, which chose me before thy father, and before all his house, to appoint me ruler over the people of the LORD, over Israel: therefore will I play before the LORD"* (II Samuel 6:21). This attitude of praise and joy reflected his gratitude for the breakthroughs in his life.

3. *Moving Forward with Renewed Vision and Purpose*
Once the breakthrough is received, it is essential to move forward with a renewed vision and purpose. This is not merely about celebrating what has happened but about using the breakthrough as a springboard for greater things ahead.

- *Seek God for New Purpose:* Breakthroughs often reveal new opportunities and callings. It is vital to seek God's guidance in how to steward this breakthrough and the new doors that are now open. The Bible encourages us to rely on God for wisdom in all things: *"If any of you lack wisdom, let him ask of God, that giveth to all men liberally, and upbraideth not; and it shall be given him"* (James 1:5, ESV).
- *Set New Goals with God's Direction:* Moving forward requires setting new goals that align with God's vision for our life. This means actively seeking out ways to use the breakthrough for His glory and for the benefit of others. Jesus said, *"The thief cometh not, but for to steal, and to kill, and to destroy: I am come that they might have life, and that they might have it more abundantly"* (John 10:10). A renewed purpose focuses on moving forward with intentionality to create a life that honors God.
- *Trust in Holy Spirit for Empowerment:* Do not attempt to move forward in your own strength. Holy Spirit empowers believers to fulfill God's purpose in their lives. *"But you will receive power when the Holy Spirit has come upon you, and you will be my witnesses in Jerusalem and in all Judea and Samaria, and to the end of the earth"* (Acts 1:8, ESV).

Example:

As referenced earlier, Apostle Paul experienced a dramatic breakthrough on the road to Damascus. His life was radically changed, and he immediately sought to understand God's new vision for him. Paul moved forward with renewed purpose, sharing the gospel, and establishing churches all over the Roman Empire. His breakthrough did not stop with salvation;

it led to a whole new direction for his life. Our breakthrough should send us onto a new trajectory as well.

Breakthroughs are significant, but they are only the doorway of new journeys. Embracing change, maintaining a heart of gratitude, and moving forward with a renewed sense of purpose are crucial to receiving and sustaining the breakthrough. When we respond to God's goodness with faith, gratitude, and vision, we position ourselves for even greater things in His kingdom.

If you desire God to usher you into and through your breakthrough, pray this prayer.

Heavenly Father,

You are the God of the impossible, the one who makes a way when there seems to be no way. I come before you today, weary but hopeful, trusting that you hear my cry. I bring to you every barrier, every burden, every closed door, and every silent battle I face. I lay them at your feet.

Lord, I ask for a divine breakthrough. Break through the chains of fear, doubt, and discouragement. Breakthrough in my circumstances where I have seen delay, disappointment, or defeat. Where there has been dryness, let rivers of living water flow. Where there has been silence, speak life. Where doors have been shut, open them by your power.

I choose to stand in faith, believing you are working even when I cannot see it. Strengthen my heart to wait on you with expectation, not anxiety. Align my will with yours and prepare me to walk through the doors you open.

Thank you, Lord, for not being distant. You are near, active, and able. My breakthrough is not found in striving but in surrender. So here I am, Lord. I trust you, I believe you, and I receive all You have for me.

In Jesus' mighty name,
Amen

My Breakthrough

A quiet prayer, a heart laid bare,
In shadows deep, a whispered prayer.
The weight of doubt, the chains of fear,
Are lifted high, when God draws near.

The storm within, a raging sea,
Finds calm when Christ steps close to me.
A flicker faint, a distant light,
Becomes a blaze that clears the night.

A voice that calls, "Come, follow me,"
And in that call, I am set free.
The past erased, the future bright,
In Christ alone, I find my might.

A soul once bound in sin's deep hold,
Now rises strong, now stands so bold.
For grace has poured, and peace has come,
A breakthrough found through God's own Son.

No longer lost, I see the way,
In every dawn, a brighter day.
A spirit healed, a heart restored,
In Him I trust, in Him I soar.

Dr. C.

NOTES

NOTES

NOTES

NOTES

NOTES

Chapter Two

Walking in Your Healing

Chapter Two
Walking in Your Healing

Healing is discussed on a regular basis amongst people all over the world. Daily, people earnestly seek healing for various ailments from medical personnel (physicians and nurses) and via online forums, such as mayoclinic.com and webmd.com. Additionally, in faith, believers pray for healing. With this topic's popularity, two questions arise: What is healing, and how is it manifested? Healing is the reversal of a condition that caused someone to be impaired, lacking perfect health. Healing can be manifested in a variety of forms: emotional, physical, mental, and spiritual. Regardless of the form, healing is manifested by God Almighty, for He is Jehovah Rapha, the God who heals.

Emotional healing is the process of acknowledging, allowing, accepting, integrating, and processing painful life experiences and strong emotions. It may involve empathy, self-regulation, self-compassion, self-acceptance, and mindfulness. Physical healing refers to the restoration of a person's physical health and well-being, encompassing the repair of damaged tissues, organs, and the biological system as a whole to resume normal functioning. Mental healing encompasses the process of addressing and resolving emotional distress, trauma, or mental health challenges to promote well-being and recovery. Spiritual healing encompasses restoration and wholeness, encompassing physical, emotional, and spiritual well-being, achieved through faith in Jesus Christ and the power of Holy Spirit.

According to the Holy Bible, it is the will of God for mankind to walk in healing, always. God is the same yesterday, today, and forevermore (Hebrews 13:8). Therefore, His nature and will have not changed. So, if God wants us to prosper and be in good health even as our soul prospers (III John 1:3), why do we constantly require healing? Why is it something for which believers are constantly praying? Why is there "laying on of hands" (Mark 16:18) in faith that the person will no longer be afflicted with an unhealthy condition?

To answer these queries, we must go back to the Garden of Eden where the fall of man occurred after Eve was beguiled by the serpent, Satan. Before the fall of man, there was no sickness on earth. There is none in heaven, and thus, sickness cannot come from heaven. So, if sickness does not come from God, from where does it come? According to Romans 5:12, *"Wherefore, as by one man sin entered into the world, and death by sin; and so death passed upon all men, for that all have sinned."* Because of sin, God permits all kinds of things to happen in the earth until He brings to pass the full redemption of the entire earth from the curse which man has brought upon it.

As a result of sin entering the world, the devil brought sickness and disease as a contrived plan to destroy God's creation - man. John 10:10 tells us, *"The thief cometh not, but for to steal, and to kill, and to destroy: I am come that they might have life, and that they might have it more abundantly."* Satan binds people with pain and disease. Therefore, sickness, disease, pain, and death are from the devil, not from God.

Conversely, Jesus came to give back to man what was stolen from him. Jesus came to bring back health and abundant life, not only in the world to come, but for now as well. Jesus destroyed the power of the enemy, so the devil's works would not overwhelm us. Jesus heals and delivers us from the snares of the enemy. Jesus brings life and healing to every believer. Isaiah 53:5 informs us, *"But he was wounded for our transgressions, he was bruised for our iniquities: the chastisement of our peace was upon him; and with his stripes we are healed."* As a result of Jesus' suffering, we gained all manner of healing (emotional, mental, physical, and spiritual) and restoration. *"He healeth the broken in heart, and bindeth up their wounds"* (Psalm 147:3).

While there are many ways healing is demonstrated and manifested to us, one way to receive healing is via FAITH. Faith comes from hearing God's Word (Romans 10:17). Jesus spoke of the person's faith in the majority of the individual cases of healing we find in the gospels. He made comments such as, "according to your faith be it done unto you," or "your faith has made you whole," or "as you have believed, so be it unto you." These comments let us know God still honors faith, and faith is still the vehicle by which we receive God's promises. We must learn to ACT on God's Word.

Let's take a look at a few biblical and modern-day examples of healing.

Biblical Examples of Healing

Throughout Scripture, God reveals Himself as a healer, who is compassionate, powerful, and deeply personal. The Bible is filled with stories of men and women who encountered God in their pain and were completely transformed. These accounts are more than historical moments; they are testimonies of God's unchanging nature and His desire to bring wholeness to every area of our lives. In this section, we will look at some of the most powerful examples of healing in the Bible, stories that not inspire faith.

Woman Thou Art Loosed

Luke 13:10-17 shares the healing account of an unnamed woman who suffered from a physical ailment for eighteen years.

> *"And he [Jesus] was teaching in one of the synagogues on the sabbath. And, behold, there was a woman which had a spirit of infirmity eighteen years, and was bowed together, and could in no wise lift up herself. And when Jesus saw her, he called her to him, and said unto her, Woman, thou art loosed from thine infirmity. And he laid his hands on her: and immediately she was made straight, and glorified God. And the ruler of the synagogue answered with indignation, because that Jesus had healed on the sabbath day, and said unto the people, There are six days in which men ought to work: in them therefore come and be healed, and not on the sabbath day. The Lord then answered him, and said, Thou hypocrite, doth not each one of you on the sabbath loose his ox or his ass from the stall, and lead him away to watering? And ought not this woman, being a daughter of Abraham, whom Satan hath bound, lo, these eighteen years, be loosed from this bond on the sabbath day? And when he had said these things, all his adversaries were ashamed: and all the people rejoiced for all the glorious things that were done by him."*

The story is brief, but it speaks volumes about healing, freedom, and compassion. The story begins with this sentence: Jesus was teaching in a synagogue on the Sabbath. Then Luke tells us a woman was there. For eighteen years, she had been crippled by a spirit. She was bent over, completely incapable of standing erect. We do not know the woman's name, but Jesus <u>saw</u> the woman. He noticed her. In the synagogue in those days, the men sat in the front, and the women sat in the back. There was complete segregation of the sexes. Yet, Jesus looked past all the men and focused on the woman among all the other women.

What did Jesus do next? He called to her. Did He know her name? How did she know He was calling her and not someone else? Somehow, she knew He was calling her. So, she went to Him.

When they were in close proximity, Jesus laid His hands upon her and said, *"Woman, you are set free of your infirmity."* He touched her despite the cultural restrictions of His day that would frown upon that action. His words and touch did not give her power or prestige, but freedom and dignity! She slowly began to stand up straight. For the first time in years, she was looking someone in the face. And, it was the face of Jesus. And what is the first thing she did with her new-found freedom? She gave glory to God! Despite her years of suffering, she knew how to give thanks to God!

Witnessing the miracle, the people were amazed at what they had just witnessed. Unsurprisingly, the leader of the synagogue was indignant because Jesus had cured on the Sabbath. But, he did not confront Jesus directly. Instead, he took the cowardly way and scolded the woman and his congregation: *"There are six days when work should be done. Come on those days to be cured, not on the Sabbath day."* In other words, when faced with a mystery he could not explain, he resorted to enforcing the rules - which he knew so well.

What was the Lord's response? Jesus became angry. He yelled: *"Hypocrites!"* Then, he revealed the insanity of the leader's remark. He continued by saying: Common sense says you untie your ox or ass on the Sabbath and lead it to water. This daughter of Abraham, whom Satan has bound for eighteen years now, ought she not to have been set free on the Sabbath day from this bondage? This woman is a daughter of Abraham. She is one of us. She is a valuable member of the faith community. She has a role to play in God's plan of salvation. (Jesus' response here is paraphrased.)

Jesus restored the woman's dignity. He set her free.

The following three accounts all come from the Book of Matthew Chapter 8 and are found in direct succession as Jesus drives forward the point of His God-given authority to heal. These examples occurred after He taught before great multitudes, particularly delivering The Sermon on the Mount as recorded in Matthew 5-7.

Leper Cleansed and Restored

Matthew 8:1-4 shares the healing account of a man afflicted with leprosy.

"When he [Jesus] was come down from the mountain,

Leper Restored
Mathew 8:1-4

great multitudes followed him. And, behold, there came a leper and worshipped him, saying, Lord, if thou wilt, thou canst make me clean. And Jesus put forth his hand, and touched him, saying, I will; be thou clean. And immediately his leprosy was cleansed. And Jesus saith unto him, See thou tell no man; but go thy way, shew thyself to the priest, and offer the gift that Moses commanded, for a testimony unto them."

In Matthew's gospel, he regularly uses the phrase *"And behold"* when he introduces something new in a narrative to which he wants to draw our attention. What are we to *behold* and wonder at in this particular passage of scripture? *"A leper came."* Picture the scene. Crowds of men, women, and children surrounded Jesus. Then, suddenly a commotion broke out in the multitude. The sea of people began to part as a poor, disheveled leper thrust his way toward Jesus. From the crowd, there might have come angry murmurs or fearful shrieks as the leper's sudden presence interrupted the scene.

Why? Leprosy was a feared disease because there was no cure. It was considered as difficult to heal from leprosy as to raise someone from the dead (II Kings 5:7). To make matters worse, while the physical symptoms of the disease were terrible, the social stigma was even worse. The Old Testament commanded that if a man contracted leprosy, *". . . His clothes shall be torn and his head bare; and he shall cover his mustache, and cry, 'Unclean! Unclean!' He shall be unclean. All the days he has the sore he shall be unclean. He is unclean, and he shall dwell alone; his dwelling shall be outside the camp"* (Leviticus 13:45-46). According to these verses, lepers were shunned. People hid themselves when a leper came into town begging for food for fear of being afflicted themselves.

Furthermore, people viewed leprosy as a curse from God, which is understandable. When Aaron and Miriam (Moses' brother and sister) spoke against Moses' authority from God, Miriam was struck with leprosy (Numbers 12:10). Gehazi, the prophet Elisha's servant, was struck with leprosy because he sought to abuse Elisha's ministry to gain material wealth for himself (II Kings 5:27). King Uzziah was struck with leprosy when he pridefully disobeyed God and sought to make an offering in the temple that was only right for the priests to make (II Chronicles 26:16-21). Because of these accounts, leprosy was viewed as a punishment from God.

Jesus' response to the leper is so beautiful as he showed compassion and the ability to heal. In Matthew 8:3, it says, *"Jesus put out His hand and touched him."* Don't miss that important point. In those days, no one touched a leper! The Old Testament warns if someone touches an unclean person or thing, that person also becomes unclean. Leviticus 5:3 says, *"Or if he touches human uncleanness - whatever uncleanness with which a man may be defiled, and he is unaware of it - when he realizes it, then he shall be guilty."* Nevertheless, Jesus did not cleanse the leper first and then touch him. He touched him while he was still a leper and then cleansed him.

Why did Jesus touch him? We know from other healing accounts that Jesus did not need to touch in order to heal. He had the authority and power to just speak a word and bring healing from a distance, establishing His word. Most likely, Jesus touched the leper to show His compassion. What a picture of God's love! Touching the leper would make a person unclean, but with Jesus the opposite happened. Instead of Jesus becoming unclean, the leper is made clean.

Jesus said to the leper: *"I am willing; be cleansed."* And that is exactly what happened! The leprosy that covered his entire body was all gone in an instant. That is the power of Christ demonstrated in this miracle. Jesus has the power to make clean in an instant, absolutely clean. With that miracle, Matthew wants us to see that Jesus is the Christ, the Son of God.

After the leper was cleansed, Jesus said to him, *"See that you tell no one; but go your way, show yourself to the priest, and offer the gift that Moses commanded, as a testimony to them."* Jesus had just worked a great miracle to cleanse the man, yet He told him not to tell anyone but to go to the priest. Why? Mainly out of obedience to the law. The law of God given through Moses states when a man was healed of leprosy, he was to go to the temple and show himself to the priests. And if, upon examination, the man indeed was healed, he was to undergo a ceremonial ritual of cleansing (Leviticus 14:1-20). Only after the ceremony had been completed by the priest could the man then be restored to the social life of his people.

Jesus was often accused of breaking the law, but His actions in this situation was a testimony that Jesus honored the law and encouraged others to honor the law, too. Jesus said in Matthew 5:17, *"Do not think that I came to destroy the Law or the Prophets. I did not come to destroy but to fulfill."* Furthermore, when Jesus supposedly broke the law, the ceremonial law had not yet been fulfilled. The ceremonial law would not be fulfilled until Jesus went to the cross. Therefore, He would honor it until it had been fulfilled upon His death.

Servant Healed of the Palsy

Matthew 8:5-13 shares the healing account of a centurion's servant who was afflicted with the palsy.

> *"And when Jesus was entered into Capernaum, there came unto him a centurion, beseeching him, And saying, Lord, my servant lieth at home sick of the palsy, grievously tormented. And Jesus saith unto him, I will come and heal him. The centurion answered and said, Lord, I am not worthy that thou shouldest come under my roof: but speak the word only, and my servant shall be healed. For*

I am a man under authority, having soldiers under me: and I say to this man, Go, and he goeth; and to another, Come, and he cometh; and to my servant, Do this, and he doeth it. When Jesus heard it, he marvelled, and said to them that followed, Verily I say unto you, I have not found so great faith, no, not in Israel. And I say unto you, That many shall come from the east and west, and shall sit down with Abraham, and Isaac, and Jacob, in the kingdom of heaven. But the children of the kingdom shall be cast out into outer darkness: there shall be weeping and gnashing of teeth. And Jesus said unto the centurion, Go thy way; and as thou hast believed, so be it done unto thee. And his servant was healed in the selfsame hour."

Servant Healed
Matthew 8:5-13

The centurion was obviously a Gentile as he was an officer in the Roman army. Most every Jew under Roman occupation felt a reason to hate the centurion, yet he went to a Jewish teacher for help. Significantly, he came not for a selfish reason, but on behalf of his servant. Whenever the New Testament mentions a centurion (there are at least seven), it presents them as honorable, good men. This centurion had an unusual attitude toward his slave. Under Roman law, a master had the right to kill his slave, and it was expected he would do so if the slave became ill or injured to the point where he could no longer work.

Jesus did not hesitate to decide to go to the centurion's house even though it was completely against Jewish custom for a Jew to enter a Gentile's house. However, it was *not* against God's law. The centurion shared his knowledge of the custom when he said, *"Lord, I am not worthy that You should come under my roof."* Most Jews believed a Gentile home was not worthy of them, and the centurion supposed that a great rabbi and teacher like Jesus would consider his home unworthy. The centurion also showed great sensitivity to Jesus, in that he wanted to spare Jesus the awkward challenge of whether or not to enter a Gentile's house as well as the time and trouble of travel. He did not know Jesus well enough to know He would *not* feel awkward in the least.

The centurion fully understood Jesus' healing power was not some sort of magic trick that required the magician's presence. Instead, he knew Jesus had true *authority* and could command things to be done and completed outside His immediate presence. The centurion's words demonstrated great faith in Jesus' word. He understood Jesus can heal with His word just as easily as with a touch.

The centurion also had first-hand information on the military chain of command and how the orders of one in authority were unquestioningly obeyed. He saw Jesus had *at least* that much authority. The man's understanding of Jesus' spiritual authority made Jesus marvel. His simple confidence in the ability of Jesus' mere word to heal showed a faith that was free of any superstitious reliance on merely external things. That was truly great faith, worthy of praise.

Jesus considered the faith of the Gentile centurion and thought it to be greater than any faith He had seen among the people of Israel. The fact that such faith was present in a Gentile caused Jesus to announce that there would be Gentiles in the kingdom of heaven. They will even sit down to dinner with Abraham, Isaac, and Jacob! This was a radical idea to many of the Jewish people in Jesus' day, for they had assumed the great Messianic banquet would have no Gentiles, and that *all* Jews would be there. Jesus corrected both mistaken ideas.

These few words of Jesus tell us a little something of what heaven is like.
- It is a place of good company to sit with; we will enjoy the friendship of Abraham, Isaac, and Jacob in heaven.
- It is a place with many people; Jesus said many will come into heaven.
- It is a place with people from all over the earth; from the north, south, east, and west, they will come to heaven.
- It is a certain place; Jesus said many will come, and when Jesus says it will happen, it will happen.

As well, Jesus reminded his Jewish listeners that just as the Gentile's racial identity was no automatic barrier to the kingdom, *their* racial identity was no guarantee of the kingdom.

Mother-in-Law Healed of Fever

Matthew 8:14-15 shares the healing account of a woman afflicted with fever.

"And when Jesus was come into Peter's house, he saw [Peter's] wife's mother laid, and sick of a fever. And he touched her hand, and the fever left her: and she arose, and ministered unto them."

Peter's Mother-in-Law
Matthew 8:14-15

This healing account is shared not only in Matthew's gospel but also in both Mark's and Luke's. Drawing from all three accounts, it is clearly ascertained that Jesus engages in healing the woman, either by hovering over her or by a gentle touch of His hand (a slight variance in the gospels). Whether or not He touched her is irrelevant. The important and most notable fact is her sickness immediately dissipated. While the woman is unnamed, her story demonstrates the power and love of Jesus.

The event took place on the Sabbath day, which is a holy day, and according to Jewish law, people were not allowed to work, which included performing miracles. After leaving the synagogue, many of the men who were worshipping went with Jesus to Simon Peter's house and were planning to eat together.

In those days, the woman of the house typically prepared the meal for the men, but the woman of that house, Simon Peter's mother-in-law, was extremely ill. Although it is not known exactly what her illness was, the Scripture says she had a very high fever, making the woman weak.

What did Jesus do? He took the woman's hand. Immediately, the fever was gone, and there was no sign of the weakness that might be expected in a person who had been running a fever. After Jesus rebuked the woman's fever, it left her, and she began to wait on the guests.

What also is notable about this miracle was Jesus 'rebuked' the fever. We see the word 'rebuke' on several other occasions, including the miracle to end the storm on the Sea of Galilee when He 'rebuked' the wind and rain, as well when Jesus 'rebuked' the demon during the exorcism in the synagogue. The word means "to censure or admonish." There are times when the solutions to our problems may require rebuke or strong admonition. No one enjoys being on the receiving end of a rebuke, yet if healing is to occur, sometimes it takes a strong word or a strong will.

Anyone can play a vital part in God's plan. The Lord's miracles in our lives are often quiet and ordinary. It is the small miracles that are performed behind closed doors that allow ordinary people to lead lives pleasing to the Lord, to serve Him, and show others His love.

Issue of Blood Removed

Mark 5:25-34 shares the healing account of a woman who was afflicted with an issue of blood.

"And a certain woman, which had an issue of blood twelve years, and had suffered many things of many physicians, and had spent all that she had, and was nothing bettered, but rather grew worse, when she had heard of Jesus, came in the press behind, and touched his garment. For she said, If I may touch but his clothes, I shall be whole. And straightway the fountain of her blood was dried up; and she felt in her body that she was healed of that plague. And Jesus, immediately knowing in himself that virtue had gone out of him, turned him about in the press, and said, Who touched my clothes? And his disciples said unto him, Thou seest the multitude thronging thee, and sayest thou, Who touched me? And he looked round about to see her that had done this thing. But the woman fearing and trembling, knowing what was done in her, came and fell down before him, and told him all the truth. And he said unto her, Daughter, thy faith hath made thee whole; go in peace, and be whole of thy plague."

Woman Cleansed
Mark 5:25-34

The story of this woman takes place within a larger story. Jesus was on His way to Jairus' (a synagogue leader) house to heal his dying daughter (Mark 5:21–24) when an unnamed woman causes an interruption to His progress. What we know about the woman is, first, she had a bleeding condition, and the issue had continued for twelve years. That is a very long time.

Second, she had spent all her money on treatments from many doctors, and nothing had helped. In fact, the blood issue had only grown worse (Mark 5:25–26).

Jewish law declared her to be ceremonially unclean due to her bleeding issue (Leviticus 15:25-27). That meant she would not have been permitted to enter the temple to attend Jewish religious ceremonies. According to the Law, anything or anyone she touched became unclean as well. The fact that she was in the crowd pressing around Jesus means that each person who bumped into her would have become unclean, too - including Jesus. But, after twelve years of suffering, she was obviously desperate for a miracle. When she heard about Jesus, she came up behind him in the crowd and touched his cloak, because she thought, *If I just touch his clothes, I will be healed.*

As soon as the woman touched Jesus, her bleeding stopped, and she knew she had been healed. In an instant, Jesus did what no doctor in twelve years had been able to do. That act proved the power of Christ, but it also illustrates an important point about Jesus and the Law. In Leviticus 15:31, God says, *"You must keep the Israelites separate from things that make them unclean, so they will not die in their uncleanness for defiling my dwelling place, which is among them."* In the Old Testament, the temple was where God dwelt among the Israelites, but in the New Testament, God dwelt among men in the person of Jesus the Christ (John 1:14). Through Jesus, the penalties of the Law are reversed, and the contamination of this world had no effect on Christ. The woman did not make Jesus unclean. Instead, He made her clean!

When Jesus felt the woman's touch, He immediately responded. People were pushing and pressing into Him from all over, yet He stopped, turned, and asked, *"Who touched my clothes?"* (Mark 5:30). The disciples were incredulous, but

Jesus knew that healing power had gone out of Him. Eventually, the woman came forward and explained herself. Jesus cleared up any misconceptions about her healing, saying, *"Daughter, your faith has healed you. Go in peace and be freed from your suffering"* (Mark 5:34). God is moved to action by our faith, even when He is in the middle of doing something else!

Jesus could have healed the woman and kept on walking to His original destination. Only He and the woman would have known what had taken place. But, He did not do that. Jesus stopped what He was doing and acknowledged the result of the woman's faith: her complete and instantaneous healing. Hallelujah!

Modern-Day Healing Examples

While the pages of Scripture are filled with powerful accounts of divine healing, God's miraculous touch did not end in ancient times. He is still healing today, physically, emotionally, and spiritually. In this section, you will read real-life testimonies of individuals who encountered the healing power of God in deeply personal ways. These stories serve as living proof that Jesus is the same yesterday, today, and forever, and that His healing hand is still at work in the world around us.

Overcoming Grief After a Loss

Gerald lost a loved one, and the weight of his grief became an ever-present burden. In the days that followed his loss, Gerald experienced deep emotional pain, struggling to make sense of the empty space left behind. Nights were often sleepless, and memories of his loved one surfaced unexpectedly, bringing both sorrow and

> **Gerald's Emotional Healing**

bittersweet comfort. Feelings of anger, confusion, and profound sadness washed over him, making even the simplest tasks seem overwhelming.

Yet, with time, Gerald took small steps toward healing. He sought therapy, where he found a safe space to express his thoughts and process his emotions. The therapist guided him through the complex layers of grief, helping him understand healing did not mean forgetting. Support from friends and family also played a crucial role in his healing process. They listened without judgment, shared memories, and reminded him that he did not have to face the pain alone.

Gerald's faith also became a source of strength. Through prayer, reflection, and the words of Scripture, he found solace in the belief that his loved one was at peace. Trusting in God's comfort and presence, he began to release some of the heaviness he carried. Each day, the sharpness of his sorrow softened, making room for moments of gratitude and remembrance.

As he navigated the path of emotional healing, Gerald learned to honor the memory of his loved one in meaningful ways. He celebrated the person's life by revisiting cherished places, sharing stories, and keeping traditions alive. Though the ache of loss remained, it no longer defined his existence. Instead, it became a reminder of the deep love he had experienced - a love that continued to shape and guide him.

Healing, Gerald realized, was not about moving on but about moving forward. He embraced life once again, knowing his loved one's presence would forever remain in his heart.

Bible Verses:
- Psalm 34:18 (NIV) – *"The Lord is close to the brokenhearted and saves those who are crushed in spirit."*

- Matthew 5:4 (NIV) – *"Blessed are those who mourn, for they will be comforted."*

Recovery From an Illness

Brenda was diagnosed with cancer, and the news shook her to her core. Fear, uncertainty, and worry flooded her thoughts as she faced the daunting road ahead. Determined to fight, she worked closely with her medical team to develop a treatment plan that included chemotherapy. Each session brought its own set of challenges, and the physical toll of nausea, fatigue, and hair loss weighed heavily on her body and spirit. Despite the discomfort, Brenda remained resolute, drawing strength from the unwavering support of her loved ones.

Brenda's Physical Healing

Throughout her journey, her faith became a source of comfort and resilience. She leaned on prayer, scripture, and moments of quiet reflection, finding solace in knowing she was not alone in her struggle. Her church community also offered words of encouragement and practical support, from meal delivery to simply sitting by her side during difficult days.

Brenda's medical team, including oncologists, nurses, and therapists, provided compassionate care, guiding her through each stage of treatment. They answered her questions, managed her symptoms, and celebrated small victories along the way. Her trust in their expertise gave her confidence that she was receiving the best possible care.

In addition to medical treatment, Brenda made intentional choices to support her body's healing. She embraced a balanced, nutritious diet, incorporating foods rich in vitamins and antioxidants. Gentle exercises like walking and yoga helped her maintain strength and combat fatigue. Mindfulness practices and relaxation techniques also eased her anxiety, allowing her to find moments of peace during the storm.

As the months passed, Brenda experienced a gradual recovery. Follow-up scans and tests brought hopeful news, and the side effects of treatment slowly subsided. Though the road had been long and arduous, she emerged with a newfound appreciation for life. Cancer had tested her in unimaginable ways, but it also revealed her resilience, faith, and the depth of her support system.

Now, Brenda continues to prioritize her health, attending regular check-ups and nurturing her body through mindful choices. She shares her story with others facing similar battles, offering hope and encouragement. Her experience serves as a testament to the power of faith, modern medicine, and the determination of the human spirit to heal and thrive.

Bible Verses:
- James 5:15a (NIV) – *"And the prayer offered in faith will make the sick person well; the Lord will raise them up."*
- Isaiah 53:5 (NIV) – *"But he was pierced for our transgressions, he was crushed for our iniquities; the punishment that brought us peace was on him, and by his wounds we are healed."*

Breaking Free From Anxiety

Jason had battled anxiety for as long as he could remember. The relentless cycle of worry and fear often left him feeling powerless, from his mind racing with worst-case scenarios. Even in moments of calm, a lingering sense of dread would creep in, making it difficult to fully enjoy life. Sleepless nights and tense

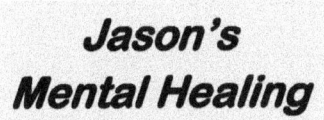

days became his norm, and he struggled to break free from the grip of his anxious thoughts.

Determined to find relief, Jason took the courageous step of seeking help. He began therapy with a compassionate counselor who created a safe space for him to express his feelings without judgment. Through their sessions, Jason explored the root causes of his anxiety and learned to recognize the triggers that intensified it. Cognitive Behavioral Therapy (CBT) equipped him with practical tools to challenge negative thought patterns and replace them with more balanced, constructive perspectives.

In addition to therapy, Jason adopted coping strategies to manage his anxiety on a day-to-day basis. Mindfulness practices became a cornerstone of his routine. By focusing on the present moment through breathing exercises and guided meditation, he found moments of calm in the midst of mental turmoil. Grounding techniques helped him reconnect with his surroundings when intrusive thoughts threatened to overwhelm him.

Jason also leaned into his faith, turning to prayer as a source of comfort and strength. He spent quiet moments reflecting on Scripture, finding reassurance in the promises of God's peace. Through prayer, he released his burdens, trusting he was not alone in his struggles. He also joined a faith-based support group, where he connected with others who understood the challenges of living with anxiety. Their shared experiences offered encouragement and reminded him healing was possible.

Gradually, Jason noticed a shift. The once all-consuming fear no longer dictated his every thought. While moments of anxiety still surfaced, he now had the tools to navigate them.

He reminded himself emotions were temporary, and he no longer viewed them as insurmountable obstacles.

Finding freedom from anxiety did not mean the absence of fear but rather the ability to face it with resilience and trust. Jason's journey taught him to embrace imperfection, practice self-compassion, and lean on his faith for strength. Through mindfulness, prayer, and continued growth, he now lives with a renewed sense of peace - a peace that no longer wavers in the face of uncertainty.

Bible Verses:
- Philippians 4:6-7 (NIV) – *"Do not be anxious about anything, but in every situation, by prayer and petition, with thanksgiving, present your requests to God. And the peace of God, which transcends all understanding, will guard your hearts and your minds in Christ Jesus."*
- II Timothy 1:7 (NIV) – *"For God hath not given us the spirit of fear; but of power, and of love, and of a sound mind."*

Mental healing in this case involved leaning into God's peace and taking practical steps to address anxiety, including therapy and support.

Restoring Faith After Doubt

Sabrina had always considered her faith a steady anchor in her life. Yet, without warning, she found herself drifting into a season of spiritual dryness. Prayers that once brought her comfort now felt empty, as though her words disappeared into silence. The familiar sense of God's presence seemed distant, leaving her with unsettling questions. Was He truly listening?

Did He care? Doubts crept into her heart, and she wrestled with feelings of confusion, guilt, and frustration.

Sabrina's Spiritual Healing

The routines of her faith: attending church, reading scripture, and singing worship songs, no longer stirred her spirit. Even moments of joy were tainted by a lingering emptiness. Sabrina felt isolated in her struggle, hesitant to admit her doubts to others. She worried about questioning her faith, thinking it might be seen as a sign of weakness.

Eventually, longing for clarity and peace, Sabrina took a step toward healing. She began to pray again, though her words were often simple and hesitant. Instead of seeking immediate answers, she prayed for the strength to endure the uncertainties. Slowly, she returned to Scripture, allowing the Psalms and the stories of biblical figures who had faced doubt and despair to speak to her heart. She took comfort in knowing she was not alone - even heroes of faith had endured spiritual deserts.

Seeking guidance, Sabrina confided in a trusted spiritual mentor. With patience and compassion, her mentor listened without judgment. He reminded her that questioning was not a sign of failure but a natural part of spiritual growth. Through their conversations, Sabrina learned to be honest with God about her feelings. She began journaling her thoughts and prayers, finding relief in putting her doubts into words.

Over time, subtle shifts took place. While the answers did not come all at once, Sabrina experienced moments of clarity via a specific verse that resonated deeply, a conversation that sparked renewed hope, and a sense of peace during a morning walk. She also discovered the importance of rest and solitude, allowing herself space to listen rather than striving to control her spiritual journey.

As Sabrina continued to seek God, her trust was gradually restored. She no longer demanded certainty but embraced the mystery of faith. The questions that once plagued her became opportunities to grow in understanding and reliance on God's presence. Through prayer, scripture, and the support of her mentor, she emerged from her season of doubt with a renewed sense of purpose and connection with Him.

Her experience deepened her empathy for others navigating spiritual dryness. Now, Sabrina walks with a quiet confidence, knowing that even in moments of silence, God is near - patiently guiding, listening, and drawing her closer to His heart.

Bible Verses:
- Jeremiah 29:13 (NIV) – *"You will seek me and find me when you seek me with all your heart."*
- Psalm 51:10 (NIV) – *"Create in me a pure heart, O God, and renew a steadfast spirit within me."*

Spiritual healing involves restoration through seeking God and His Word and being open to His transformative presence and process.

Mending a Broken Friendship

Denise and Gayle had been friends for years, sharing laughter, tears, and countless memories. They were each other's confidantes - the kind of friends who could finish each other's sentences and knew when something was wrong with just a glance. But one

Denise & Gayle's Relational Healing

day, a misunderstanding shattered that bond. A careless remark, a misinterpreted action, and assumptions left unchecked created a rift between them. Hurtful words were exchanged, and resentment took root. The warmth of their friendship was replaced with awkward silences and avoidance.

Both women felt the weight of the fractured relationship. Denise replayed the conversations in her mind, wondering if she could have responded differently. Gayle wrestled with feelings of betrayal and disappointment, unsure if reconciliation was even possible. Pride and fear held them back from reaching out, and the distance between them grew wider.

Yet, amidst the pain, neither could forget the deep friendship they had once shared. Through prayer and reflection, both Denise and Gayle began to feel a gentle prompting - a call to forgive. They were reminded that true healing requires humility and vulnerability. Denise prayed for the strength to let go of bitterness, while Gayle asked God for the courage to listen and understand.

Finally, Denise reached out with a heartfelt message, expressing her desire to talk. Gayle, though hesitant at first, agreed. They met at a quiet café, both anxious but determined. As they sat across from each other, the walls of resentment began to crumble. Honest words flowed - not accusations, but sincere reflections on the hurt they had both experienced. Denise apologized for the ways she had contributed to the pain, and Gayle acknowledged her own regrets.

Through tears and shared understanding, they chose to forgive. It was not an instant fix, but a conscious decision to rebuild what had been broken. They leaned on their faith, trusting God to heal the wounds that lingered. With time, they restored the trust that had been lost, offering one another grace and patience.

Their friendship, though once fractured, became even stronger. Denise and Gayle now approached their relationship with greater empathy and wisdom. They understood the importance of clear communication, of giving the benefit of the doubt, and of extending forgiveness not as a sign of weakness, but as an act of strength and love.

Through God's guidance, their friendship stood as a testament to the power of reconciliation. And with each passing day, they cherished their bond anew - grateful for the grace that had brought them back together.

Bible Verses:
- Matthew 18:21-22 – *"Then Peter came to Jesus and asked, 'Lord, how many times shall I forgive my brother or sister who sins against me? Up to seven times?' Jesus answered, 'I tell you, not seven times, but seventy-seven times.'"*
- Ephesians 4:32 – *"Be kind and compassionate to one another, forgiving each other, just as in Christ God forgave you."*

Relational healing emphasizes the power of forgiveness and reconciliation, which fosters growth and restoration in relationships.

Do You Require Healing?

You may need healing if you experience persistent patterns of emotional pain, unhappiness, or dissatisfaction in various areas of your life or if you notice a lack of emotional regulation or self-compassion. These signs along with others listed below may suggest you require healing. Read through them with an open mind, assessing yourself honestly.

Repetitive Patterns of Pain or Unhappiness

If you find yourself repeatedly stuck in cycles of dissatisfaction - whether in work, relationships, or life in general, it could be a sign of unhealed emotional wounds. These patterns often manifest as recurring conflicts, persistent feelings of unfulfillment, or making the same choices that lead to disappointment and frustration.

Unresolved pain from past experiences can shape our behaviors, perceptions, and decisions in ways we may not fully realize. For example, a history of betrayal may lead to a fear of trust, causing difficulties in forming meaningful relationships. Childhood experiences of neglect or criticism might result in seeking validation through unhealthy work habits or staying in toxic environments or relationships.

These cycles are often rooted in subconscious beliefs we carry about ourselves and the world. Without recognizing and addressing them, we may unknowingly recreate situations that mirror past wounds. The discomfort we experience is not just random. Rather, it serves as a signal, urging us to examine the deeper emotional layers beneath our struggles.

Breaking free from these patterns requires self-reflection, emotional awareness, and intentional healing. Therapy, journaling, meditation, and spiritual growth can help uncover the origins of these repetitive struggles. By identifying the emotional wounds driving our behaviors, we can begin the process of healing, fostering healthier choices and relationships.

True transformation happens when we confront the pain, learn from it, and allow ourselves to grow beyond it. Healing is not about erasing the past but about rewriting how it shapes our present and future. When we take steps toward emotional restoration, we break the cycle and open ourselves to a life of greater peace, fulfillment, and authentic happiness (rather than manufactured or coerced happiness).

Difficulty with Emotional Regulation

Struggling to manage emotions, feeling easily triggered, or having difficulty expressing needs and boundaries are strong indicators of unhealed emotional wounds. Emotional regulation is the ability to recognize, process, and respond to emotions in a healthy and balanced way. When this ability is compromised, emotions may feel overwhelming, unpredictable, or difficult to control.

Unhealed wounds from past experiences, such as childhood trauma, unresolved grief, or repeated rejection from friends or loved ones, can make emotional responses more intense or disproportionate to present situations. You may find yourself reacting impulsively, experiencing sudden bursts of anger or sadness, or shutting down emotionally as a form of self-protection. Small conflicts may feel like personal attacks, and feedback may trigger deep feelings of inadequacy or shame. When you experience these emotions and have these responses, it is important to quickly ascertain the reason for the response, such as having your defenses up in situations when it is not warranted.

Difficulty with emotional regulation can also lead to challenges in communication and relationships. You might struggle to articulate your needs, thoughts and emotions, fearing rejection or conflict, or you may have trouble setting boundaries, either allowing people to overstep or becoming overly defensive. This can create cycles of frustration, misunderstandings, and emotional exhaustion.

Healing in this area involves self-awareness, emotional processing, and intentional self-care. Therapy, mindfulness practices, and emotional regulation techniques, such as deep breathing, grounding exercises, and cognitive reframing, can help develop a healthier relationship with emotions. Learning to pause before reacting, identifying emotional triggers, and practicing self-compassion are all key steps in gaining control over emotional responses.

With time and effort, emotional healing fosters resilience, balance, and a greater sense of inner peace. It allows you to experience emotions fully without being consumed by them, communicate effectively, and establish healthier relationships with yourself and others. Healing is not about suppressing emotions but learning how to navigate within them with wisdom and grace. Further, it is important to surround yourself with people who demonstrate compassion and understanding as you navigate your season of healing.

Lacking Self-Compassion

Being overly critical of yourself, struggling to forgive your mistakes, or feeling unworthy of love and acceptance can be strong indicators of unhealed emotional wounds. Self-compassion is the ability to extend kindness, understanding, and patience to yourself, just as you would to a close friend or loved one. When this is lacking, your inner dialogue may be filled with self-judgment, feelings of inadequacy, or an inability to move past failures and regrets. Instead, strive to speak encouragingly to yourself. You deserve kindness, love, respect, and gentleness – from yourself as well as from others.

This struggle often stems from past experiences - perhaps harsh criticism in childhood, unrealistic expectations placed upon you, or painful moments where you felt unworthy. Over time, these experiences can shape your self-perception, leading you to believe you must be perfect to be valued or that mistakes define your worth. The inability to forgive yourself may also be tied to guilt, shame, or the fear that you are undeserving of grace.

Without self-compassion, you may push yourself too hard, set unattainable standards, or avoid taking risks due to fear of failure. You might find it difficult to accept compliments, downplay your achievements, or feel unworthy of love and kindness from others. This inner struggle can contribute to anxiety, depression, and a general sense of dissatisfaction with life, which are all detrimental to your mental health and stability for the remaining course of your life.

Healing in this area involves recognizing your worth is not tied to perfection or performance. Practicing self-kindness, challenging negative self-talk, and embracing your humanity are crucial steps. Therapy, journaling, affirmations, and mindfulness can help reframe how you see yourself. Learning to offer yourself the same grace you extend to others allows for growth, inner peace, and a deeper sense of self-acceptance.

True healing happens when you realize you are enough - not because of what you do, but simply because you exist. Embracing self-compassion is not self-indulgence. It is the foundation for emotional resilience, healthier relationships, and a more fulfilling life.

Physical Symptoms

Experiencing persistent physical ailments or pain without a clear medical cause can be a strong indicator of unresolved emotional issues. The mind and body are deeply connected, and unprocessed emotional pain often manifests physically. Stress, anxiety, and suppressed emotions can trigger real, tangible symptoms that may not have an obvious medical explanation.

Common physical signs of emotional distress include chronic headaches, muscle tension, digestive issues, unexplained fatigue, or even frequent colds due to a weakened immune system. Sleep disturbances, such as insomnia or restless nights, can also stem from unresolved inner turmoil. In some cases, emotional pain may contribute to conditions like high blood pressure or heart palpitations.

When emotional wounds remain unhealed, the body often carries the burden. Trauma, grief, or long-term stress can activate the body's fight-or-flight response, keeping it in a heightened state of alertness. Over time, this prolonged stress can wear down the nervous system, leading to physical exhaustion, tension, and discomfort.

Healing these physical symptoms requires addressing not only the body but also the emotions and experiences behind them. Mindfulness, relaxation techniques, and therapy can help release stored emotional pain. Practices like deep breathing, yoga, and meditation can calm the nervous system and promote healing. Expressing emotions (through journaling, creative outlets, or seeking professional support) can also help alleviate physical manifestations of emotional distress.

Recognizing the link between emotional health and physical well-being is a crucial step toward healing. When we take care of our emotional wounds, we often find relief not just in our hearts and minds but in our bodies as well. True healing happens when both emotional and physical needs are acknowledged, nurtured, and restored.

Reliving Past Trauma

If you find yourself constantly reliving past traumatic experiences, it may be a sign that your mind and body are still holding onto unresolved pain. Trauma has a way of imprinting itself deeply into our psyche. When left unprocessed, it can resurface in various forms: flashbacks, nightmares, emotional triggers, or an overwhelming sense of fear and distress. These experiences may feel as vivid and painful as when they first occurred, making it difficult to move forward.

Reliving trauma can manifest in different ways. You may find yourself replaying painful memories in your mind, unable to let them go. Certain sounds, smells, places, or even seemingly unrelated situations might trigger intense emotional or physical responses, such as anxiety, panic attacks, or a sense of detachment. You may also experience avoidance, causing you to subconsciously steer clear of anything that reminds you of the trauma, even if it limits your ability to fully engage with life. This is when the trauma takes control of your life.

Unprocessed trauma can affect relationships, self-esteem, and daily functioning. It may lead to heightened stress responses, difficulty trusting others, emotional numbness, or cycles of self-blame. Over time, this can take a toll on both mental and physical well-being.

Healing from trauma requires acknowledging its impact and allowing yourself the space to process it in a healthy way. Seeking professional support, such as therapy or trauma-informed counseling, can provide tools to work through painful memories in a safe and structured manner. Practices like mindfulness, journaling, and praying can help release stored trauma and restore a sense of safety and control. By facing and processing past trauma with patience and support, you can reclaim your peace, find emotional freedom, and step into a future that is not defined by past pain but by resilience and hope.

Difficulty Bouncing Back from Adversity

If you struggle to cope with setbacks or disappointments, or if challenges leave you feeling overwhelmed and emotionally drained, it may be a sign that deeper healing is needed. Resilience - the ability to adapt and recover from hardship - is an important aspect of emotional well-being. When resilience feels out of reach, it may indicate unresolved pain, self-doubt, or past wounds that make it difficult to navigate life's ups and downs.

Unhealed emotional wounds can make even minor setbacks feel insurmountable. You may find yourself stuck in a cycle of self-doubt, fear, or frustration, questioning your ability to handle difficulties. Past experiences of failure, rejection, or loss may have created a sense of helplessness, making it hard to trust in your own strength or in the possibility of better days ahead. Instead of viewing obstacles as temporary challenges, they may feel like confirmation of deep-seated fears of inadequacy or unworthiness.

Difficulty bouncing back from adversity can also stem from a lack of self-compassion. If you hold yourself to unrealistic standards or fear making mistakes, setbacks can trigger harsh self-judgment rather than an opportunity for growth. This can lead to avoidance, procrastination, or even self-sabotage, preventing you from taking risks or pursuing new opportunities.

Healing in this area involves building emotional resilience by addressing past wounds, shifting your mindset, and developing healthy coping mechanisms. Seeking support from a therapist, mentor, or supportive community can provide valuable perspective and encouragement. Mindfulness, self-care, and reframing negative thoughts can also help you see challenges as opportunities for growth rather than as evidence of failure. Remember, not everything in life will be easy or go as you have planned. Challenges will arise, so allow the challenges to make you stronger rather than causing you to retreat and become easily defeated.

True healing allows you to face adversity with confidence, knowing that setbacks do not define you. True healing empowers you to rise stronger, wiser, and with a renewed sense of hope. When healing takes place, resilience becomes not just an ability but a source of strength that carries you forward, no matter what challenges come your way.

Feeling Stuck or Unfulfilled

If you feel like you are not living up to your potential or your life lacks purpose, that may be a sign that underlying emotional or psychological wounds need attention. Feeling stuck in your career, relationships, or personal growth can stem from unresolved fears, limiting beliefs, or past disappointments that have shaped your self-perception and decision-making.

This sense of stagnation may manifest as a deep dissatisfaction with your daily routine, a lack of motivation, or an inner restlessness that no external success seems to satisfy. You might find yourself asking the following questions: *Is this all there is?* or *Why do I feel unfulfilled despite having everything I thought I wanted?* These feelings can be frustrating, especially if you cannot pinpoint exactly what is holding you back.

Often, past experiences, such as criticism, failure, or unmet expectations, can create mental roadblocks that prevent you from fully stepping into your purpose. Fear of failure, perfectionism, or self-doubt may keep you from taking risks or pursuing passions that once excited you. Additionally, unresolved emotional pain can drain your energy and keep you from embracing new opportunities, leaving you feeling trapped in cycles of routine and predictability.

Healing in this area requires deep self-reflection and a willingness to explore the root causes of your stagnation. Practices such as journaling, therapy, meditation, or seeking spiritual guidance can help uncover hidden fears and clarify your true desires. Reconnecting with your passions, setting small goals, and embracing change can reignite a sense of purpose and direction. Surrounding yourself with supportive people who inspire and challenge you can also be a powerful catalyst for growth.

True fulfillment comes not from external achievements alone but from aligning your life with your values, passions, and authentic self. Healing allows you to move past internal roadblocks and step into the life you were meant to live - one filled with purpose, joy, and a renewed sense of possibility.

Changes in Behavior or Relationships

Significant shifts in your behavior or relationships, such as becoming more withdrawn, irritable, or controlling, can be signs that deeper emotional wounds need attention. When unresolved pain lingers beneath the surface, it often manifests in the way we interact with ourselves and those around us. These changes may not always be obvious at first, but over time, they can impact personal connections, work dynamics, and overall well-being.

Withdrawal from social interactions, for example, may stem from feelings of unworthiness, fear of vulnerability, or emotional exhaustion. You might avoid loved ones, cancel plans, or feel disconnected even when surrounded by people. On the other hand, increased irritability may be a sign of suppressed emotions - anger, grief, or frustration - that has not been processed properly. Small inconveniences or minor conflicts may trigger strong emotional reactions, leaving you feeling overwhelmed, hurt, or guilty.

Some individuals may cope with emotional wounds by becoming more controlling, whether in personal relationships or daily routines. This can stem from a deep-seated fear of uncertainty or past experiences where they felt powerless. By trying to control situations, people, or outcomes, they seek a sense of security and predictability, often at the expense of their own peace and the well-being of those around them.

Recognizing these behavioral changes is an important step toward healing. Instead of dismissing them as personality shifts or external stress, it helps to reflect on their underlying causes. Are you avoiding people because of past hurt? Are your emotional reactions disproportionate to situations? Are you trying to control things out of fear rather than genuine need?

Healing in this area involves self-awareness, emotional regulation, and a willingness to address root causes. Therapy, journaling, and open conversations with trusted friends or mentors can provide insight and support. Practicing mindfulness, self-compassion, and healthy coping strategies can also help restore emotional balance.

When healing occurs, relationships become healthier, interactions feel more genuine, and emotional reactions become more measured. Instead of allowing past wounds to dictate your behavior, you regain the ability to engage with life and others in a way that is authentic, peaceful, and fulfilling.

The Healing Process

IF after reading the last section and noticing you have many of the traits mentioned, it may be time to navigate through your personal healing journey.

Embracing the Journey of Healing - Why It Takes Time

Healing is not a quick fix or a one-time event. It is a journey that unfolds over time as well as one that may require repeating throughout one's life. Just as physical wounds take time to mend, emotional and spiritual wounds likewise require patience, gentleness, and intentional care. There will be ups and downs, including moments of clarity and peace, followed by times of struggle and setbacks. Although the downs may not feel great, there occurrence is normal. True healing involves unlearning patterns that may be engrained into your psyche, confronting painful truths that may have gone unrealized, and gradually rebuilding a healthier relationship with yourself and others. It is a process that cannot and should not be rushed. Embracing the journey means accepting where you are right now, without judgment, and trusting growth is happening, even when progress feels slow or invisible. Healing is not about perfection. Rather, it is about movement, no matter how small, in the direction of wholeness. The only way you can walk in your authenticity is by becoming whole.

The Importance of Surrendering to God for Healing

At the heart of true healing is the willingness to surrender. Often, we try to manage our pain on our own by staying busy, numbing out, pretending everything is fine, or attending to others' needs. Essentially, we go through the motions of a healthy, healed person while being broken or damaged within. But healing becomes deeper and more transformative when we surrender our wounds to God, inviting Him into the very places we cover up from public view. Often times, we have only dealt with what lies directly on the surface of our countenance. However, many wounds are deeply imbedded within us, sometimes deeper than we know.

God's love is gentle, patient, and redemptive. When we surrender to Him, we outwardly acknowledge we cannot do it all on our own and we need His strength to carry us through. Surrender is not about giving up or being weak. It is about letting go of control and trusting God's timing, wisdom, and grace to lead us through the process. It is in this place of dependence that true restoration begins. While we may find no one who understands what we are confronted with, there is at least one who understands – the Lord, and He will graciously walk us through the process.

How to Embrace Vulnerability and Openness in the Healing Process

Healing requires vulnerability - the courage to be honest about where you hurt, what you fear, and what you need. This openness can feel risky, especially if you have been wounded in the past. But vulnerability is the gateway to connection, growth, and emotional freedom. Being open with trusted people - a counselor, mentor, or safe community - can provide comfort, perspective, and support. It also creates space for God to work through others in your life. Vulnerability with God means bringing Him your raw, unfiltered emotions - your doubts, your anger, your questions - knowing He can handle it all. When you allow yourself to be seen and known in your brokenness, healing flows more freely. Vulnerability is not weakness. It is the strength to show up authentically and say, "This is where I am, God. Meet me here."

Together, these steps - embracing the journey, surrendering to God, and opening yourself to vulnerability - form the foundation of meaningful, lasting healing.

Signs of Emotional Healing

When you detect change within yourself in any of the areas mentioned earlier (in the section *Do You Require Healing?*), healing has begun to take place. Now, you will begin to notice many of the positive aspects discussed below.

- *You allow yourself to feel your emotions.*

When you are in survival mode, you focus on logic and keeping busy. You know if you slow down or take your eye off logic, emotions – both the ones that feel good and the ones that feel bad – will remind you of pain. It is easier and less painful to keep the painful memories and emotions buried. However, when you begin to heal, you recognize it is crucial to acknowledge and feel your emotions, even when it hurts. This means you may also be giving up being overly busy. In doing this, you understand the importance of acknowledging and feeling your emotions, particularly the "bad" ones, allowing them to rise to the surface, so you can address them in a healthy manner.

- *You express and maintain boundaries more effectively.*

When you are not emotionally healed, it is really hard to communicate and uphold boundaries because you believe it will lead to rejection, conflict, and guilt from prioritizing your own needs. In healing, you start to learn that while you still do not like or want conflict, rejection or guilt, you can handle them. You begin to see you are allowed to say what you need and want and that it is essential to speak up, even if it feels uncomfortable or may lead to conflict. This leads to healthier interpersonal dynamics and creates an environment where your opinions and emotions are valued because you externally demonstrate that you value yourself.

- *You accept that you have been through really painful situations.*

Life can be tough and unjust, and you have been through some difficult times. You know you are healing when you integrate those experiences into your life story rather than suppress, deny, or on the flip-side, overly accentuate your painful experiences. You acknowledge that those experiences shaped you. When you do this, you have taken control of your life story.

- *You become more self-aware of your own reactivity.*

In survival mode, everything and everyone can seem like a threat. To cope with this, you adopt a defensive stance where there is no time to think things through. This hyper alert state leads to lashing out, shutting down, running away, or people-pleasing. However, when we begin to heal, we develop an awareness that we do this and start to question ourselves by asking: "Why do I do this?" or "Why do I think like this?" When there is more self-awareness, it paves the way for self-regulation, analysis, and ultimately, taking responsibility for your actions.

- *You realize the healing process is not linear.*

During the healing process, there are ups, downs, progressions, and regressions, making the process recursive rather than linear. It is uncomfortable to confront suppressed emotions and memories. When wounded, you avoid them because you believe the emotions and memories will swallow you up and never let you go. However, with practice, you realize experiencing distress is temporary and not only a normal part of the healing process, but also in life. As a result, your distress tolerance window widens, giving you room to explore healthy coping strategies.

- *You no longer cling to your comfort zone.*

In tandem with an improved distress tolerance, you develop a sense of confidence that allows you to take calculated steps out of your comfort zone. You are braver and more courageous. A willingness to leave your comfort zone opens you up to new experiences and people, increased creativity and strength, and keeps the personal development going. You will probably also want to make a change to your surroundings. You will want your environment to match your improved mood.

- *You cope better with disappointments.*

Life is a rollercoaster of ups and downs, with both successes and failures. Prior to healing, disappointments can feel crushing and drain all your motivation and passion. However, once you have started the healing journey, you begin to realize bad days are unavoidable, but they do not last forever. As a result, you become less reactive to negative situations and more accepting of life's balance.

- *You have more inner peace.*

You begin to accept all parts of yourself: the good, the bad, and the ugly. You no longer criticize yourself as harshly. And, this new perspective allows you to forgive yourself and others, while reducing the likelihood of self-sabotage and self-criticism. Outward signs of inner peace can be subtle, such as sleeping better or singing along in the car.

- *You are not opposed to help.*

Survivors of trauma tend to have a sense of hyper competency and autonomy. It is no surprise. Those are the very coping skills that allowed you to survive whatever awful situation you were in. While it is admirable to be independent, it is important to recognize the value of help and support. The "don't ask for help" mentality of an independent survivor is outdated and unhelpful. As strong as you are, there will be times when you need assistance. Remember, it is not your responsibility to carry heavy burdens alone. Jesus told us to cast our burdens upon Him, for His yoke is easy and His burdens are light (Matthew 11:28-30).

After reading this entire chapter, I hope you now realize that despite our broken, hurt, and unhealthy condition, we can go to Jesus with confidence and receive His healing from all that ails us. He will touch us and gently usher us into and through our healing process, if we allow Him. Jesus heals the same way He saves: through our willingness to surrender our lives unto to Him. He is the Great Physician, and He has the antidote.

If you desire God's healing virtue in your life, pray this prayer.

Heavenly Father,

You are the Lord who heals - Jehovah Rapha, the one who sees every wound and knows every pain. Today, I come before you seeking your healing touch. You know the burdens I carry, the battles within my body, mind, and spirit. Nothing is hidden from you, and nothing is beyond your power to restore.

I ask you, Lord, to bring healing where there is brokenness, peace where there is anxiety, and strength where there is weakness. Whether you choose to heal instantly, gradually, or through your divine wisdom in unexpected ways, I trust in your goodness and timing.

Let your presence be my comfort. Let your Word be my anchor. And let your love be the balm that soothes every affliction. I receive your healing by faith, not because I am worthy, but because Jesus already bore my sickness and pain on the cross. By His stripes, I am healed.

Thank you for being near to the brokenhearted and faithful to heal what is broken. I place my healing in your hands and rest in the assurance of your care.

In Jesus' name,
Amen

A Journey to Healing

I wandered through shadows, lost and afraid,
A heart worn thin, a spirit frayed.
The weight of sorrow, doubt, and fear,
A silent ache both far and near.

I searched for answers, grasping air,
A restless soul in deep despair.
Yet even in my trembling cry,
A gentle voice was drawing nigh.

"Come as you are," the voice whispered,
"Lay down the burdens that you have held.
For every tear, for every scar,
I've seen your pain - I know how far."

In quiet prayer, I spoke my name,
Admitting weakness, disappointment, and shame.
And through the stillness, mercy flowed,
A light within the dark bestowed.

The walls I built began to fall,
Replaced by grace that covered all.
Each wound I bore, each fear I fed,
He touched with love and healed instead.

No longer bound by chains unseen,
My spirit soared - restored, serene.
Through storms that pass and skies that clear,
I walk in peace, for He is near.

A journey long, a story told,
From brokenness to life made whole.
And though the road winds ever on,
My soul is held - I am not gone.

Dr. C.

NOTES

NOTES

NOTES

NOTES

NOTES

Chapter Three

Activating the Power of Restoration

Chapter Three
Activating the Power of Restoration

When many of us think of restoration, we tend to think of something or someone being restored or repaired. However, restoration is more than just repair. It is the act of bringing something or someone back to life, to the original design, or even to a better version of what once was. In the spiritual sense, restoration reflects God's desire and ability to renew what has been damaged, lost, or forgotten. Whether it is a broken heart, a fractured relationship, a dream that has faded over time, or a sense of identity and purpose that has been clouded by life's hardships, God's restoration is complete, intentional, and deeply personal for the individual.

In this chapter, we will journey through the many facets of divine restoration. We will begin by understanding the biblical foundation of restoration and how it reflects the very nature of God, understanding He is not only a Redeemer but also a Restorer. From the lives of individuals in Scripture who were restored after failure or loss to modern-day testimonies of healing and renewal, you will see how restoration is woven throughout God's story for humanity. What He accomplished in biblical times can be accomplished today. Malachi 3:6 declares, *"For I am the LORD, I change not..."* and Hebrews 13:8 says, *"Jesus Christ the same yesterday, and to day, and for ever."*

We will also explore how restoration applies to different areas of life, including relationships that have suffered from betrayal or distance, dreams that were once full of passion but are now buried under disappointment, and personal purposes that have been derailed by fear, shame, or distraction. Each area reveals a unique dimension of God's love and His desire to bring wholeness where brokenness once existed.

This chapter will also guide you in preparing your heart for restoration. We will discuss the importance of surrender, repentance, forgiveness, and hope as vital steps in making space for God to move. Restoration often begins with a willingness to believe again, trust again, and let God rebuild what we may have thought was beyond repair.

Finally, we will define what it means to experience full restoration - not just the return of what was lost, but a renewal that comes with fresh vision, deeper strength, and a testimony that glorifies God. This chapter will encourage you to see your wounds not as the end of your story, but as the starting point for something beautiful, something made whole by God's hands, which are loving and restoring.

I. Restoration Via a Biblical Lens

When we look at restoration through a biblical lens, we see a consistent theme of God taking broken people, shattered situations, and ruined places, and bringing about renewal for His glory. From the lives of Job, Joseph, and Peter to the redemptive work of Christ, Scripture reveals that God specializes in restoring what sin, suffering, or time has damaged. In this section, we will explore how the Bible defines and demonstrates the restorative power of God.

A. *The Biblical Concept of Restoration*

In Scripture, restoration is not just about repair; it is about *renewal, redemption,* and *divine recompensing.* Restoration is rooted in the very heart of God. God's restoration is thorough and overflowing. In Joel 2:25 (ESV), the Lord promises, *"I will restore to you the years that the swarming locust has eaten..."* This verse speaks to more than just physical loss; it points to God's power to redeem time, experiences, and opportunities that were seemingly wasted or stolen. Similarly, in Jeremiah 30:17 (NIV), God declares, *"But I will restore you to health and heal your wounds.'"* He is reaffirming that He sees our pain and is actively working to bring healing and wholeness.

Both verses reveal restoration is not only an act. Restoration is reflective of God's character. He is the Restorer. Where there has been destruction, He brings rebuilding. Where there has been sorrow, He brings joy. Where there has been loss, He brings replenishment in abundance.

B. *God's Desire to Restore All Things*

Often times, we limit God's ability in our mind by not fully conceptualizing Him in His complete capacity. With that in mind, understand restoration is not limited to isolated areas of our lives. Do not limit God's ability to bring restoration in your life by failing to understand His omnipotence. God desires to restore *all things* - our dreams, our health, our relationships, our identity, and even our faith. Maybe, we have let go of dreams because of disappointment. Maybe, our relationships have suffered from misunderstanding, betrayal, or distance. Perhaps, our physical health has been a constant battle or our hope has been dimmed by life's burdens. Whatever the case, God is not blind to what has been broken. Nor is He blind to what the enemy has stolen from us. His heart is to restore every part of our lives, completely and lovingly.

The restoration God offers is not <u>only</u> about returning what once was, but about leading us into what could be - into something richer, stronger, and more deeply rooted in His purpose for us. Restoration is about moving forward, not backward. It is about transformation, not duplication or replication.

C. Restoration as a Divine Promise and Plan

God does not restore because He feels pity for us. He restores because it is part of His divine promise and redemptive plan for humanity. Throughout the Bible, we see a continuous theme of restoration. From the Garden of Eden (Genesis) to the ministry of Jesus (the Gospels) to the promise of a new heaven and new earth (Revelation), God is always in the business of reclaiming what has been lost.

His promises are clear and consistent: If we turn to Him, trust Him, and open our hearts, He will bring restoration. This includes not just physical or emotional healing but also spiritual renewal and renewed purpose. What the enemy meant for harm, God turns around for good (Genesis 50:20). The cracks in our lives become places where His light shines through most beautifully.

> *"You intended to harm me, but God intended it for good to accomplish what is now being done, the saving of many lives."*
> Genesis 50:20

In this chapter, we will dive deeper into how to walk in the reality of God's restorative promises. You will see that no matter how broken something may seem, with God, restoration is always possible. Remember, *"With men this is impossible; but with God all things are possible"* (Matthew 19:26). And, it is often even more glorious than what you originally had in mind. Ephesians 3:20 tells us, *"Now unto him that is able to do exceeding abundantly above all that we ask or think, according to the power that worketh in us."*

II. God Restores in Multiple Areas

Restoration is not limited to one aspect of life; it touches everything. When God restores, He restores *wholly* - mind, body, soul, and spirit. In this section, we will explore key areas where God desires to bring renewal and healing.

A. *Restoration of Dreams*

Many of us carry dreams that were once alive but have unfortunately faded. Whether due to fear, failure, or circumstances outside our control, we often bury the desires God once placed in our hearts. But God never forgets what He has planted in us. In fact, restoration means He can breathe new life into old dreams - or give you fresh ones that align with who you have become through your journey. Psalm 37:4 says, *"Delight yourself in the Lord, and He will give you the desires of your heart."* When you draw close to Him, your dreams can be restored - not only revived but refined.

B. *Restoration of Relationships*

Broken relationships are one of the deepest sources of pain but also one of the most beautiful areas for God's redemptive work. Whether it is a marriage strained by hurt, a friendship shattered by misunderstanding, or a family bond weakened by distance, God specializes in reconciliation. II Corinthians 5:18 reminds us that God has given us the "ministry of reconciliation," and it starts with Him. When we invite God into our relationships, He not only heals but strengthens them, often bringing more depth and grace than they ever had before.

> *"All this is from God, who reconciled us to himself through Christ and gave us the ministry of reconciliation."*
> II Corinthians 5:18 (NIV)

C. Restoration of Health

God also cares deeply about our physical and emotional well-being. Though He does not always heal in the way or timing we expect, He does promise to walk with us through every valley. In Jeremiah 30:17 (NIV), God says, *"But I will restore you to health and heal your wounds."* Healing may come through divine intervention, medical wisdom, lifestyle changes, or emotional growth, but in every step, God is present, offering strength, comfort, and hope.

D. Restoration of Purpose and Identity

Life has a way of distorting our sense of self and confusing our sense of purpose. Through trauma, rejection, failure, or even success, we may forget who we are in God's eyes. But part of restoration is remembering you were created for a reason and with a purpose to be fulfilled in the earth. Ephesians 2:10 (NLT) says, *"For we are God's masterpiece. He has created us anew in Christ Jesus, so we can do the good things he planned for us long ago."* You are not forgotten. God desires to restore your sense of identity and renew your confidence in the unique calling on your life.

E. Restoration of Joy and Peace

Lastly, God desires to restore what often goes unnoticed but deeply impacts our daily lives: our joy and peace. Life's hardships can dull our sense of wonder, steal our laughter, and replace rest with worry. But Romans 15:13 (NIV) reminds us,

"May the God of hope fill you with all joy and peace as you trust in Him..." God wants to restore your inner world, not just your outer circumstances. He desires that you live not just healed, but whole - carrying a peace that surpasses understanding and a joy that cannot be shaken by the circumstances we encounter.

III. Biblical Examples of Restoration

Throughout Scripture, the theme of restoration emerges as a powerful testimony to God's unwavering love, mercy, and redemptive power. Time after time, we see individuals and entire nations fall into sin, suffering, or in despair, only to be lifted, healed, and restored by the hand of God. These stories are more than historical accounts. They are divine reminders that no situation is too broken for God to redeem. From the fall of man in the Garden of Eden to the resurrection of Jesus Christ, the Bible is filled with vivid portraits of restoration that reveal God's heart to renew what has been lost. In this section, we will explore key biblical narratives that showcase how God restores lives, relationships, purpose, and promise, offering us hope for our own journey of restoration.

Job's Tragic Loss- Restored in Abundance

The story of Job is one of the most profound and moving accounts of suffering and restoration in the Bible. Job was a man of great wealth, integrity, and deep devotion to God. Yet, in a matter of moments, everything he held dear was stripped away. The book of Job portrays not just a physical and emotional tragedy, but also a spiritual journey, one that ultimately ends in divine restoration.

Job's Tragic Loss
Job 1:13-21; 42:10, 16-17

In the early chapters, we see Job face unimaginable loss. He lost his livestock, his servants, his home, and, most painfully, all of his children. The devastation was delivered in waves, with each messenger bringing darker news than the last. The chaos unfolds in Job 1:13-19, where we read:

> *"One day when Job's sons and daughters were feasting and drinking wine at the oldest brother's house, a messenger came to Job and said, 'The oxen were plowing and the donkeys were grazing nearby, and the Sabeans attacked and made off with them. They put the servants to the sword, and I am the only one who has escaped to tell you!' While he was still speaking, another messenger came and said, 'The fire of God fell from the heavens and burned up the sheep and the servants, and I am the only one who has escaped to tell you!' While he was still speaking, another messenger came and said, 'The Chaldeans formed three raiding parties and swept down on your camels and made off with them. They put the servants to the sword, and I am the only one who has escaped to tell you!' While he was still speaking, yet another messenger came and said, 'Your sons and daughters were feasting and drinking wine at the oldest brother's house, when suddenly a mighty wind swept in from the desert and struck the four corners of the house. It collapsed on them and they are dead, and I am the only one who has escaped to tell you!'"*

This avalanche of tragedy would break even the strongest of hearts. And yet, Job's response is breathtaking in its humility and reverence. Read Job 1:20-21:

> *"At this, Job got up and tore his robe and shaved his head. Then he fell to the ground in worship and said: 'Naked I came from my mother's womb, and naked I will depart.*

> *The LORD gave and the LORD has taken away; may the name of the LORD be praised.'"*

Despite his grief, Job did not sin or accuse God of wrongdoing. Instead, he entered into a posture of worship - a profound declaration of trust in the sovereignty of God, even amidst despair. Throughout the book, Job wrestled with deep questions of suffering, justice, and the silence of God. He was visited by friends who misjudged his situation, offering misguided counsel and false assumptions. Still, Job remained steadfast, pouring out his heart in lament and longing for answers. Then, in the final chapter - Job 42:10 - everything shifted.

> *"After Job had prayed for his friends, the LORD restored his fortunes and gave him twice as much as he had before..."*

That moment marked the turning point. God not only restored what Job had lost. He blessed Job double. Job's brothers and sisters returned to him, offering comfort, silver, and gold. His material possessions were multiplied:

- 14,000 sheep
- 6,000 camels
- 1,000 yoke of oxen
- 1,000 donkeys

But the restoration was not only material; it was personal and deeply relational. Job was given seven sons and three daughters, and the names of his daughters, Jemimah, Keziah, and Keren-Happuch, are specially noted, emphasizing their beauty and dignity. Unusual for the time, Job granted his daughters an inheritance alongside their brothers, a remarkable act of honor and equality. He may have been acting in accordance to the change in the traditional law Moses enacted on behalf of Zelophehad's daughters (Numbers 27).

The chapter concludes with a picture of complete restoration. Read Job 42:16-17.

"After this, Job lived a hundred and forty years; he saw his children and their children to the fourth generation. And so Job died, an old man and full of years."

This story reminds us that God is able to restore what has been lost, even beyond our understanding. Restoration does not erase the pain of the past, but it brings beauty, blessings, and meaning out of brokenness. Job's life is a testament to God's faithfulness, even in suffering, and His power to redeem every part of our lives. The story of Job goes far beyond the restoration of wealth and possessions. It reveals God's heart to redeem, restore, and renew even the most shattered aspects of our lives. It challenges us to view restoration not just as the return of what was lost, but as a divine transformation that brings new life, deeper wisdom, and greater faith.

Here are some key takeaways from Job's restoration account:

- *God Sees What You Have Lost*
  Just as God saw Job's pain, He sees yours. Whether it is the loss of a loved one, a dream that did not come to pass, a relationship that broke your heart, or a season of suffering, *God is not indifferent to your pain.* He walks with you in it, and He is already working behind the scenes to bring restoration in His time.
- *Restoration Is Not Always Immediate, But It Is Certain*
  Job's restoration did not happen overnight. He endured intense emotional, physical, and spiritual suffering. But even in his lowest moments, he remained in conversation with God, sometimes in anguish, sometimes in worship. Restoration often takes time, but God's promises never fail.

- *Restoration Often Begins with Surrender*
  Job's turning point came when he prayed for his friends, those who had misunderstood and even hurt him. This act of humility and forgiveness opened the door for God's blessing to be released. Sometimes, our restoration begins when we lay down bitterness, pride, or fear and surrender our pain into God's hands.
- *God's Restoration Multiplies, Not Just Replaces*
  When God restores, He does not simply return what was lost. He gives back more. More joy. More peace. More strength. More purpose. Job received twice as much as he had before and lived long enough to enjoy the fruits of his restoration. God's restoration brings abundance, not just survival.
- *Your Story Can Become a Testimony*
  Job's life became a source of encouragement for countless generations. Your story -your trials, your faith, your healing- can inspire and uplift others as well. Never underestimate the power of your testimony.

Joseph's Journey - From the Pit to the Palace

In Scripture, there are few stories that capture the full spectrum of human pain, betrayal, endurance, and divine restoration, such as the story of Joseph, the eleventh son of Jacob. His life, recorded in Genesis 37–50, serves as a reminder that God's plans are never derailed by human actions. In fact, they often unfold through them. From being the favored son to a forgotten prisoner, and finally to the most powerful man in Egypt under Pharaoh, Joseph's journey is a testament to God's faithfulness in every season.

> **Joseph's Journey**
> **Pit to Palace**
> Genesis 37-50

From his youth, Joseph was set apart from his brothers and despised by them. As his father Jacob's favorite son, Joseph received a coat of many colors, a symbol of honor that stirred the jealousy and hatred of his ten older brothers.

> *"Now Israel loved Joseph more than all his children, because he was the son of his old age: and he made him a coat of many colours"* (Genesis 37:3).

Adding to the tension, Joseph had prophetic dreams that foretold his future leadership, even over his family. When he shared his dream with his brothers, anger grew inside of them. What God had revealed was exciting and intriguing to Joseph, but it enraged his brothers, inciting violence in them.

> *"And Joseph dreamed a dream, and he told it his brethren: and they hated him yet the more"* (Genesis 37:5).

The brothers' jealousy led to the development of a plot. While some wanted to kill Joseph, others suggested they sell him. Ultimately, Joseph was thrown into a pit, then sold for twenty pieces of silver to traveling Ishmaelites. Afterward, they presented his bloodied coat to Jacob, who believed his beloved son was dead.

> *"And they took him, and cast him into a pit... and they sold Joseph to the Ishmaelites for twenty pieces of silver"* (Genesis 37:24, 28).

In Egypt, when Joseph was sold to Potiphar, an officer of Pharaoh, God's favor remained upon him, causing Joseph to quickly rise in the ranks to oversee Potiphar's household.

> *"And the Lord was with Joseph, and he was a prosperous man... and his master saw that the Lord was with him"* (Genesis 39:2–3).

Yet again, Joseph's integrity was tested. He resisted the sexual advances of Potiphar's wife, only to be falsely accused and imprisoned for his righteousness.

> *"And she caught him by his garment... and he fled, and got him out"* (Genesis 39:12).
>
> *"And Joseph's master took him, and put him into the prison"* (Genesis 39:20).

Even behind bars, God's presence never left Joseph. He was given leadership over other prisoners and entrusted with interpreting dreams.

> *"But the Lord was with Joseph, and shewed him mercy... and that which he did, the Lord made it to prosper"* (Genesis 39:21, 23).

Joseph interpreted dreams for Pharaoh's imprisoned butler and baker. Not long after, that connection changed Joseph's future. When Pharaoh was troubled by dreams no one could interpret, the butler remembered Joseph. Joseph was then brought before Pharaoh, and by God's wisdom, he interpreted the dreams, foretelling seven years of plenty followed by seven years of famine. Joseph was made ruler over all Egypt, second only to Pharaoh. At just thirty years old, Joseph was positioned to save Egypt and the world from famine, though he was not made aware of it yet.

> *"Thou shalt be over my house... only in the throne will I be greater than thou"* (Genesis 41:40).

During the famine, Joseph's brothers came to Egypt seeking grain. They did not recognize him, but Joseph knew them. Through emotional encounters and divine testing, Joseph ultimately revealed his identity and forgave them for their trespasses against him when he was just a teenager.

> *"I am Joseph your brother, whom ye sold into Egypt. Now therefore be not grieved... for God did send me before you to preserve life"* (Genesis 45:4–5).

He reconciled with his family and provided for them, bringing his father Jacob to Egypt where the family would be preserved.

> *"And Joseph nourished his father, and his brethren... with bread, according to their families"* (Genesis 47:12).

Joseph's story offers a striking illustration of restoration. After being sold into slavery, falsely accused, and imprisoned, he was eventually raised to power in Egypt. If Joseph had been released any sooner, he would not have been in position to save a nation from famine or reconcile with the very brothers who betrayed him. God's timing was perfect, not just for Joseph, but for everyone connected to his purpose.

Here are some key takeaways from Joseph's restoration account:

- *God is Sovereign Over Every Season*
  Whether Joseph was in a pit, a prison, or a palace, God was always working behind the scenes to fulfill His divine purpose in Joseph's life.
- *Integrity Brings Favor, Even in Adversity*
  Joseph's unwavering commitment to righteousness, especially in Potiphar's house and in prison, was honored by God, opening doors no man could shut.
- *Delay is Not Denial*
  Joseph waited over a decade between his dreams and their fulfillment. While waiting, he was being refined and prepared for his divine assignment.
- *Forgiveness Leads to Healing and Legacy*
  Joseph's choice to forgive his brothers restored a broken family and helped birth the future of the nation of Israel, saving them from extinction during the famine.

- *God Restores Better Than Before*
   Joseph lost his freedom, his family, and his homeland, but God restored it all and elevated him to greater influence than he could ever imagine.

Joseph's life is a blueprint for those navigating seasons of betrayal, delay, or hardship. His story reminds us God's plans are never hindered by the wrongs of others. On the contrary, He can use every setback as a setup for restoration. Like Joseph, if we remain faithful, God will use our pain as a pathway to purpose. And, the palace of promise will be worth every step.

"But as for you, ye thought evil against me; but God meant it unto good, to bring to pass, as it is this day, to save much people alive" (Genesis 50:20).

Peter's Transition - From Denial to Destiny
Apostle Peter, who embodied boldness and passion, was one of Jesus' most devoted followers. He was the first to declare Jesus as the Christ, the Son of the living God, and was one of the closest disciples in Jesus' inner circle. Yet, in a moment of fear and weakness, Peter did the unthinkable: He denied Jesus three times during His darkest hour, the time of His arrest that proceeded His crucifixion. But, that was not the end of Peter's story. Through Christ's grace and intentional restoration, Peter was forgiven, recommissioned, and used mightily to help build the early Church.

Peter's story is a powerful illustration of God's infinite mercy, redemptive grace, and the opportunity for restoration - even after failure. Peter had an unwavering love for Jesus. He left his fishing business to follow Him (Matthew 4:18-20), walked on water at Jesus' command (Matthew 14:29), and even declared he would die before denying Him.

> *"Peter said unto him, Though I should die with thee, yet will I not deny thee. Likewise also said all the disciples"* (Matthew 26:35).

But Jesus, knowing the human heart, warned Peter he would deny Him three times before the rooster crowed.

> *"Jesus said unto him, Verily I say unto thee, That this night, before the cock crow, thou shalt deny me thrice"* (Matthew 26:34).

When Jesus was arrested and taken to the high priest's courtyard, Peter followed at a distance. There, in the cold shadow of fear and uncertainty, Peter was confronted three times. Each time, he denied knowing Jesus.

> *"But he denied before them all, saying, I know not what thou sayest"* (Matthew 26:70).

> *"And again he denied with an oath, I do not know the man"* (Matthew 26:72).

> *"Then began he to curse and to swear, saying, I know not the man. And immediately the cock crew"* (Matthew 26:74).

The moment the rooster crowed, Peter remembered Jesus' words. The weight of his failure crushed him.

> *"And he went out, and wept bitterly"* (Matthew 26:75).

That was not just a slip of the tongue. Peter's denial was a painful betrayal of the one he loved most. After Jesus' resurrection, Peter returned to fishing, perhaps unsure of his standing with the risen Lord. But Jesus had not given up on Peter. He restored Peter not with rebuke, but with love.

> *"So when they had dined, Jesus saith to Simon Peter, Simon, son of Jonas, lovest thou me more than these?... He saith unto him, Feed my lambs"* (John 21:15).

Jesus repeats this question three times, echoing Peter's three denials, not to shame him, but to affirm him. With each answer, Jesus recommissioned Peter:

"Feed my sheep" (John 21:16–17).

Peter, broken yet beloved, is publicly restored and entrusted again with the care of Christ's followers. Peter's restoration was powerful and permanent. In Acts 2, Peter was filled with the Holy Spirit and boldly preached at Pentecost, leading 3,000 souls to salvation.

> "Then Peter said unto them, Repent, and be baptized every one of you in the name of Jesus Christ... Then they that gladly received his word were baptized: and the same day there were added unto them about three thousand souls" (Acts 2:38, 41).

The same man who had once denied Christ then proclaimed Him publicly and without fear. Peter went on to perform miracles, write Scripture, and ultimately died a martyr's death - all for the glory of the One he once denied.

Here are some key takeaways from Peter's restoration account:

- *God's Grace Is Greater Than Our Failures*
  Peter's denial did not disqualify him from God's purpose. God's grace restored him completely and used him mightily.
- *True Repentance Leads to Restoration*
  Peter's sorrow was not just emotional. It was a pivotal turning point in his life. His tears were the beginning of his transformation.
- *Jesus Seeks and Restores the Broken*
  After the resurrection, Jesus found Peter (John 21:1-17) despite Peter's denial of knowing Him. He does not

abandon us in our shame. He comes to us and reaffirms His love.

- *Your Worst Moment Is Not Your Final Chapter*
  What Peter thought was the end was actually a setup for his greatest ministry. Failure does not have to define your destiny.
- *Restoration Requires Relationship*
  Jesus did not just forgive Peter; He drew him back into close fellowship and commissioned him again. True restoration is always relational.

Peter's story speaks to every believer who has ever failed, faltered, or fallen short. His life assures us that God does not discard us when we stumble. Instead, He lovingly restores, recommissions, and reaffirms His calling over our lives. Peter became a pillar of the Church not because he was perfect, but because he was perfectly forgiven.

Jesus' Resurrection: God's Ultimate Restoration

Jesus' resurrection stands as the ultimate and most powerful expression of God's ability to restore - not only life but hope, faith, purpose, and eternal destiny. It is the foundation of the Christian faith and the proof of God's victory over sin, death, and despair.

Jesus' Resurrection
The Risen Savior
Matthew 28:1-10; Luke 24:1-12

What seemed like the end - a brutal crucifixion and a sealed tomb - became the beginning of a new era of hope, redemption, and restoration.

Jesus' death was more than a tragic loss. To His followers, it was a devastating blow to everything they had come to believe. His mother, Mary, stood in unspeakable grief. His disciples, shaken and scattered, were plagued by fear, confusion, and sorrow. The community that had followed Him, believed in His miracles, and hoped for a Messiah felt the sharp pain of disappointment and loss. Judas, one of His twelve, had betrayed Him and died in shame. The remaining eleven were left in the shadows of uncertainty.

But the story did not end in darkness.

On the third day, the same Spirit that had descended like a dove at Jesus' baptism, the same Spirit that had led Him through the wilderness and empowered His ministry, raised Him from the dead in glorious power. The resurrection was not just a miraculous event. It was the dawning of divine restoration. Where grief had taken hold, joy was birthed. Where fear once lived, peace was poured out. Where hope had been buried, it rose with Christ from the grave.

Matthew's account in Chapter 28:1–10 captures the revelation of the miracle that occurred that morning:

> *"After the Sabbath, at dawn on the first day of the week, Mary Magdalene and the other Mary went to look at the tomb. There was a violent earthquake, for an angel of the Lord came down from heaven and, going to the tomb, rolled back the stone and sat on it. His appearance was like lightning, and his clothes were white as snow. The guards were so afraid of him that they shook and became like dead men. The angel said to the women, 'Do not be afraid, for I know that you are looking for Jesus, who was crucified. He is not here; he has risen, just as he said. Come and see the place where he lay. Then go quickly and tell his disciples: "He has risen from the dead and is going ahead of you into Galilee. There you will see him." Now I have told you.' So the women hurried away from the tomb, afraid yet filled with joy, and ran to tell his disciples. Suddenly Jesus met them. 'Greetings,' he said.*

They came to him, clasped his feet and worshiped him. Then Jesus said to them, 'Do not be afraid. Go and tell my brothers to go to Galilee; there they will see me.'"

That moment was more than just a reunion; it was a revelation. The angel's greeting, simple yet profound, "Do not be afraid," echoed like a divine promise through the hearts of all who heard it. Then, His appearance was the proof that sorrow would not have the final word. Death could not hold Him, and because of that, it cannot hold us.

Luke's perspective in Chapter 24:1-12 reveals a powerful emotional truth:

"On the first day of the week, very early in the morning, the women took the spices they had prepared and went to the tomb. They found the stone rolled away from the tomb, but when they entered, they did not find the body of the Lord Jesus. While they were wondering about this, suddenly two men in clothes that gleamed like lightning stood beside them. In their fright the women bowed down with their faces to the ground, but the men said to them, 'Why do you look for the living among the dead? He is not here; he has risen! Remember how he told you, while he was still with you in Galilee: "The Son of Man must be delivered over to the hands of sinners, be crucified and on the third day be raised again."' Then they remembered his words. When they came back from the tomb, they told all these things to the Eleven and to all the others. It was Mary Magdalene, Joanna, Mary the mother of James, and the others with them who told this to the apostles. But they did not believe the women, because their words seemed to them like nonsense. Peter, however, got up and ran to the tomb. Bending over, he

saw the strips of linen lying by themselves, and he went away, wondering to himself what had happened."

The words spoken by angels clothed in radiant light struck a chord of truth that reverberated through the hearts of the women at the tomb. They remembered Jesus' words. Everything He had said - every prophecy, every promise - was all true. And they ran to tell the others, breathless with awe and bursting with joy.

Even in disbelief and confusion, as seen in Peter's response, there is a spark of restoration. Peter, the one who had denied Jesus three times, is drawn to the tomb. He peers in, sees the linen strips, and walks away in wonder. That marked the beginning of his own personal restoration - a journey that would later make him a pillar of the early church.

The resurrection is not just a historical event; it is a spiritual reality that still breathes life into us today. It is the divine declaration that no situation is beyond God's reach. Whatever has died in your life - whether it be dreams, relationships, joy, or purpose - can be resurrected by the power of the risen Christ. Through Him, restoration is not just possible; it is promised.

As you reflect on the empty tomb, remember this: God is still in the business of raising what has fallen and restoring what has been broken. Jesus lives - and in Him, so can every hope you thought was gone.

Here are some key takeaways from the account of Jesus' resurrection:
- *The Resurrection is the Pinnacle of God's Restorative Power*
  Jesus' resurrection is the ultimate proof that God can restore *anything*, even life itself. It demonstrates His

authority over death, sin, and despair, affirming that no loss is too final for God to redeem.

- *Restoration Often Follows Deep Pain and Loss*
  Before the joy of resurrection came the agony of crucifixion. Jesus' followers experienced confusion, heartbreak, and grief - emotions that mirror our own during times of brokenness. Restoration does not ignore suffering; it emerges *through* it.

- *Christ's Resurrection Revives Hope*
  Christ's resurrection turned hopelessness into hope. What seemed like the end became a new beginning, proving that God can bring beauty from ashes and light from darkness. This assures us that in our lowest moments, restoration is still possible.

- *God's Promises Are True*
  The angel's reminder, "just as He said," validates every word Jesus spoke. His resurrection affirms God keeps His promises, and what He has declared over your life will come to pass, even if it seems delayed or impossible.

- *Restoration is Both Personal and Communal*
  Mary Magdalene, Peter, and the other disciples all experienced individual moments of restoration, yet the resurrection also restored the *community* of believers. Healing may begin in our hearts, but it extends outward into relationships and purpose.

- *Fear and Joy Can Coexist*
  The women at the tomb were "afraid yet filled with joy." It is a powerful reminder that restoration does not require perfect emotional clarity. Even when fear lingers, joy and hope can still break through when we encounter the risen Christ.

- *Jesus Meets Us on the Road to Restoration*
  The post-resurrection appearances of Jesus were deeply relational. He met people *on the way*, whether on the road, at the tomb, or behind locked doors, just as He meets us where we are, in our questions, grief, or doubt.
- *Restoration Leads to Commission*
  After the resurrection, Jesus did not just comfort His followers. Instead, He commissioned them. Restoration is not the end. Rather, it is the beginning of purpose and mission. He empowers us to share the good news of redemption with others.
- *Nothing is Too Dead for God to Raise*
  If death could not hold Jesus, then no dead dream, lost hope, or broken life is beyond God's reach. His resurrection declares that your story is not over and that God specializes in reviving what others deem hopeless.
- *Restoration is Ongoing*
  Peter's story reminds us that restoration is often a journey. Though he denied Jesus, his presence at the tomb and later reinstatement by Jesus show failure is not final. God is patient, merciful, and faithful to restore over time.

IV. Modern-Day Restoration Examples

As demonstrated in the last section, the Bible is filled with powerful stories of restoration, and God still seeks to restore lives today. Restoration is not an outdated concept, meaning God's healing, redemption, and renewal are not confined to ancient times. Restoration continues in the lives of everyday people who surround us.

In this section, you will read modern-day examples of individuals who have faced deep loss, heartbreak, and brokenness; yet, they experienced the transforming power of God's grace. These modern stories serve as living proof that no situation is beyond God's reach and that His restoration is just as active and personal now as it was in Scripture. Whether it is a restored relationship, renewed faith, or a reclaimed sense of purpose, each testimony is a reminder that God can still restore what has been broken.

Sophia's Journey: From Brokenness to Wholeness

Sophia was once full of dreams. As a young woman, she had a radiant hope for her future, envisioning one shaped by purpose, love, and a deep relationship with God. She imagined herself building a family grounded in faith, working in a career that brought her joy, and serving in her church with passion and compassion. Her heart was filled with optimism, and her spirit was alive with the fire of her calling.

But life, with its unexpected turns and heavy burdens, slowly unraveled Sophia's vision. Her first deep wound resulted from a painful and unexpected divorce. The marriage she believed would last forever dissolved in a storm of betrayal and unmet expectations. In the aftermath, Sophia felt discarded and defeated. Not long after, she lost the job that had given her a sense of identity and purpose, leaving her questioning not just her abilities, but her true value. Layer by layer, she felt her world being stripped away. Her once vibrant connection to her church and faith community also began to fade. Shame, grief, and disillusionment crept in silently until she found herself severely isolated, emotionally numb, and spiritually distant.

Sophia continued to function outwardly, giving the appearance that all was well with her. Inwardly though, she was breaking. She moved through her days like a shadow of who she once was, working just to pay the bills, avoiding deep connections, and distracting herself with anything that kept her from facing the ache in her soul. She had stopped praying, stopped hoping, and stopped believing healing was possible. The fire of her faith had turned to smoldering flame that was nearly a pile of ashes.

Then, one quiet morning, quite unexpectedly, something stirred within her. It was not loud or dramatic. It was just a gentle longing for peace, something she did not realize she needed. In that stillness, she reached for her old, dust-covered Bible, the same one she used to carry with joy. With trembling hands, she opened to Psalm 23, and her eyes fell on the words: *"He restoreth my soul..."* (Psalm 23:3). The words pierced her like a light in the darkness. Her heart broke open, and she wept, not just from sorrow, but from a glimmer of hope she thought she had lost, understanding God was stepping into a space she had left reserved for only Him. At that moment, Sophia knew the Lord was ushering her into a season of peace.

That single moment became the catalyst for a new beginning. Sophia began to pray again. At first, her prayers were clumsy and ended with a tear-streaked face. Sometimes, they were just silent cries. But God met her in that sacred space. Little by little, she reached out, first to a trusted spiritual mentor, then to a small women's support group where she found safety, understanding, and encouragement. She returned to church, where she was welcomed with open arms. As she opened her heart, God began to fill it again, showing her it was okay to trust again.

She forgave those who had hurt her. She asked forgiveness from those she had shut out. She learned to forgive herself. And in that surrender, the healing power of God began to flow freely through her life. Slowly, opportunities that once seemed lost began to reappear. Doors opened that she thought had long since closed. Sophia found meaningful work again, with a deep sense of purpose and not shallow involvements. Her faith was no longer just an idea; it became her anchor. She knew unequivocally that she could lean and depend on God.

Unspeakable joy returned to her life. Not because all her problems had disappeared, but because she recognized God as her source – for everything. Isaiah 61:3 came alive in her spirit: *"To give unto them beauty for ashes, the oil of joy for mourning, the garment of praise for the spirit of heaviness..."*

Today, Sophia is a beacon of hope to others. She now mentors women walking through their own seasons of loss and despair. Her pain did not vanish, but it greatly subsided, no longer consuming her focus. What once silenced her now gives her a voice of wisdom, compassion, and grace.

> *"To give unto them beauty for ashes, the oil of joy for mourning, the garment of praise for the spirit of heaviness..."*
> Isaiah 61:3

Her story is not just a testimony of survival; it is a witness to the restoring, renewing, and redemptive power of God. Sophia's life proclaims this unshakable truth: God restores broken hearts, revives lost dreams, and reawakens destinies that seemed buried for good.

Jeff's Journey: Redemption from the Ruins

Jeff had always prided himself on being a self-made man, not relying on anyone for anything. Growing up in a tough neighborhood with little support and few opportunities, he learned early how to survive with limited resources. By the time he reached his thirties, Jeff had built what was seemingly a successful life. He owned a small business, drove a nice car, and had a reputation for being tough, driven, and in control. But behind the facade, Jeff was running on empty.

His business was crumbling under the pressure of debt and poor decisions. His marriage was unraveling from years of emotional distance and unresolved anger. And Jeff, though never one to admit weakness, was battling the weight of addiction, turning to alcohol to silence the anxiety, shame, and inner void he did not know how to fill.

The breaking point came late one Saturday night. After a heated argument with his wife, she packed a bag and left with their two children. Jeff sat alone in the silence, surrounded by empty bottles and unpaid bills. For the first time, he did not feel angry. He just felt empty, scared, and hopeless. He dropped to his knees and said out loud, "God, if you're real... I need you. I need you to show up now! If I ever needed you, I need you now!" That prayer - raw, desperate, and imperfect - became the turning point of Jeff's life.

The next morning, bright and early, he walked into a local church he had driven past a hundred times. The people there did not judge him; they welcomed him. One of the pastors invited him to coffee. That conversation led to another, and eventually to Jeff attending a recovery group held at the church. It was the first time Jeff ever shared his struggles out loud, finding he was not alone as he had felt for the last couple of years.

While attending the group meetings, Jeff started reading the Bible, and one verse seemed to echo his journey: *"If any man be in Christ, he is a new creature: old things are passed away; behold, all things are become new"* (II Corinthians 5:17). He clung to God's promise. With God's help and the support of a community he never expected to be a part of, Jeff began to change. He took responsibility for his actions. He apologized to his wife, who saw the beginnings of true repentance. Though it was a long road, they slowly started rebuilding trust. He entered counseling, got sober, and began rebuilding his business on new, honest foundation. He was thankful to have the opportunity for a new beginning without having to suffer permanent loss.

In time, Jeff became a mentor in the same recovery group that had helped save his life. He started volunteering at a local youth center, speaking to young men who, like him, felt lost and unseen. He told them his story in an effort to offer hope, explaining God does not just forgive the past; He redeems it.

Today, Jeff's life is not perfect, but it is peaceful. His marriage is strong, his children see a different man than the one he used to be, and his heart is no longer hardened by pride but softened by God's grace.

His story embodies the truth of Joel 2:25: *"And I will restore to you the years that the locust hath eaten..."* Jeff lives as a testimony that no one is too far gone, no story too broken, for God to rewrite. Restoration is not just possible; it is real. And it begins the moment we invite God into the ruins.

> *"And I will restore to you the years that the locust hath eaten..."*
> Joel 2:25

Orlando's Journey: From Incarceration to Inspiration

Orlando grew up in a neighborhood where survival took precedence over dreams. His childhood was marked by poverty, instability, and limited guidance. By his teenage years, Orlando had fallen in with the wrong crowd, and by the time he was twenty, he was serving a ten-year prison sentence for robbery. His life seemed destined for a tragic pattern of crime, punishment, and brokenness.

Behind bars, anger was his companion, and hope was a foreign concept. But something began to shift within him when a volunteer chaplain started leading Bible studies in the prison. Out of boredom and with skepticism, Orlando attended one. He did not expect much, but the chaplain's words about grace and redemption stirred something deep inside. Over time, he began reading the Bible himself, wrestling with guilt, shame, and the longing for a second chance.

A turning point came when Orlando read Romans 8:1: *"There is therefore now no condemnation to them which are in Christ Jesus."* He realized he had been carrying a sentence in his heart even greater than the one from the court, which was self-condemnation. That day, Orlando prayed for forgiveness and surrendered his life to Christ. For the first time, he felt emotionally, psychologically, and spiritually free even though his body remained in a cell.

Over the remaining years of his sentence, Orlando became a model inmate. He earned his GED, started mentoring younger prisoners, and led Bible studies. When he was finally released, he faced enormous challenges: finding work, rebuilding trust with his family, and reentering a world that had moved on. But he remained rooted in his faith, leaning on scriptures like Joel 2:25, *"And I will restore to you the years that the locust hath eaten."*

Slowly, doors began to open. A local pastor gave him a chance to work in the church's outreach program. He later became a certified counselor, specializing in youth intervention. Today, Orlando runs a nonprofit that mentors at-risk teens and provides support for formerly incarcerated individuals. His story is one of profound restoration, where guilt gave way to grace, and brokenness became a bridge to blessing.

Peaches' Journey: Healing from Abuse and Finding Her Voice

Peaches was the life of every room she entered, being warm, vivacious, and kind-hearted. But behind her bright smile was a history of hidden wounds. Raised in a home marked by emotional and physical abuse, she learned at a young age to mask pain with performance. As an adult, she continued the cycle of silence, entering a series of toxic relationships that mirrored the dysfunction she had grown up with.

Though she believed in God, Peaches often felt unworthy of His love. She struggled with self-esteem, shame, and the fear that she would never break free from the patterns of her past. Church felt like a place where she had to pretend to be okay, and eventually, she stopped going altogether, not liking the pretense of it all. She did not understand that the church is likened to a hospital, where people who need healing go.

It was not until her body began to physically break down under the weight of her emotional pain -dealing with insomnia, anxiety, and depression- that she knew something had to change. A friend invited her to a women's retreat, and though hesitant, Peaches went. There, in a moment of prayer and honesty, she broke down and confessed the years of abuse and self-doubt she had buried. The words of Psalm 147:3 came alive in that moment: *"He healeth the broken in heart, and bindeth up their wounds."*

> *"He healeth the broken in heart, and bindeth up their wounds."*
> Psalm 147:3

Peaches began therapy, joined a support group for survivors, and slowly returned to her faith community. She realized that vulnerability is not weakness; it is the beginning of healing. Through time, prayer, and community, she rebuilt her sense of identity as a beloved daughter of God.

Today, Peaches is a powerful advocate for women who have experienced trauma. She leads healing circles at her church and uses her voice to break generational cycles. Her laughter now comes from a place of authenticity, and her joy is evidence that what the enemy meant for evil, God has used for good.

Zaire's Journey: Restoring a Lost Identity

Zaire was always the one who had it all figured out, or so it seemed. A high-achieving student, driven professional, and committed volunteer, he lived a life of excellence. But beneath the surface, Zaire struggled with an unhealthy drive for perfection and an unrelenting need for approval, especially from his father, whose praise was rare and whose criticism was frequent.

As the years went by, Zaire's identity became entirely wrapped up in achievement. He measured his worth by success and feared failure like the plague. When he was unexpectedly laid off from a prestigious job he had poured himself into, Zaire was beyond devastated. Without the title or position, he did not know who he was anymore. He was unable to see himself clearly. Depression set in, and he began to withdraw from friends and family, not wanting them to detect his anguish, disappointment, and regret.

One night, while reading through old journals, Zaire found a note he had written in college after hearing a sermon on Isaiah 43:1: *"Fear not: for I have redeemed thee, I have called thee by thy name; thou art mine."* The verse pierced through his despair like light in darkness. He realized he had spent so much time trying to create an identity instead of embracing the one God had already given him.

Zaire began a journey inward, seeking God not just for what He could give but to develop a relationship with Him. He re-engaged with his church, joined a men's discipleship group, and started seeing a Christian counselor. He also began writing again, something he had loved but abandoned in pursuit of "success," not believing he could earn enough to survive.

Today, Zaire is an author and speaker, helping others detach from performance-based identity and live freely in Christ. His story reminds us that restoration is not just about recovering what was lost; it is about discovering who we truly are in God.

V. Why Restoration is Necessary

Restoration is not merely a hopeful idea. It is a divine necessity. In a world marked by pain, loss, sin, and brokenness, every person carries some form of damage in their soul, relationships, or purpose. Whether caused by the wounds of others, our own mistakes, or the unavoidable trials of life, the need for restoration is universal. It reaches beyond physical repairs and touches the deepest parts of who we are, in our hearts, minds, and spirits.

We were not created to live in a state of disrepair. From the beginning, God's desire has been wholeness - wholeness in our relationship with Him, with others, and within ourselves. Yet because of the fall of humanity, that wholeness was fractured. But here's the good news: God is not only the Creator, He is the Restorer. His heart beats for redemption, and His hands are skilled in rebuilding what was broken.

This section explores why restoration is not just helpful but absolutely essential for every believer. We will examine the condition of the human heart, the consequences of the past, and the power of divine renewal.

A. *The Impact of Loss, Brokenness, and Disrepair*

Life in a fallen world guarantees that, at some point, we will all face loss, suffering, and maybe spiritual weakness. Whether it is emotional wounds, relational breakdowns, moral failures, or unfulfilled dreams, brokenness finds us all. But in order to embrace restoration, we must first acknowledge the reality and depth of what has been lost. Throughout Scripture, brokenness is not hidden. It is exposed and explored. King David experienced the sting of moral failure and the collapse of family peace. Job lost everything and sat among ashes. Even Jesus wept over the brokenness of Jerusalem.

> *"The Lord is nigh unto them that are of a broken heart; and saveth such as be of a contrite spirit"* (Psalm 34:18).

Our brokenness, though painful, is not wasted. It becomes the very soil where God begins His work of renewal. We just have to open the door of our heart and lives to allow Him entrance to do the work in us.

> *"He healeth the broken in heart, and bindeth up their wounds"*
> Psalm 147:3

Loss humbles us and reminds us of our need for God. It brings to light what we cannot fix on our own and opens the door for divine intervention. Without recognizing our state of brokenness, we will never cry out for healing. Therefore, taking a long honest look at ourselves is imperative.

B. *How the Past Affects Our Present and Future*

The past, whether good, bad, or tragic, always leaves a mark. Traumas, disappointments, sins, and wounds often shape our identities and limit our faith in what God can do now. For many, the broken pieces of yesterday remain scattered in our heart today, interfering with joy, trust, and spiritual growth, whether those pieces are realized or not.

> *"For as he thinketh in his heart, so is he..."*
> Proverbs 23:7a

The enemy often uses our past as a weapon to imprison us in shame, fear, or bitterness. But God uses it as a canvas for redemption. Joseph was betrayed by his brothers, enslaved, and imprisoned, but looking back, he saw God's redemptive hand:

> *"But as for you, ye thought evil against me; but God meant it unto good, to bring to pass, as it is this day, to save much people alive"* (Genesis 50:20).

Even Paul, who once persecuted Christians, boldly proclaimed the transformative power of God's grace: *"But by the grace of God I am what I am: and his grace which was bestowed upon me was not in vain..."* (I Corinthians 15:10). Acknowledging the past is not about living in it. It is about surrendering it to God, so He can reshape our present and make way for our future.

C. Embracing the Need for God to Restore and Renew

True restoration begins when we recognize we cannot repair ourselves. The wounds we carry, the sins we have committed, and the years we feel we have wasted are not beyond God's reach, but they are beyond our ability to heal without Him. Restoration is not just about fixing the broken parts of our lives. It is about renewal of the soul, mind, and spirit. God does not just patch things up. He makes all things new.

> *"Create in me a clean heart, O God; and renew a right spirit within me"* (Psalm 51:10).

Restoration requires faith that God is able, willing, and ready to restore what has been lost, stolen, or destroyed. He is not intimidated by our past nor limited by our present. The Lord delights in restoring His people. When we invite God into our brokenness, we do not just find healing. We find transformation.

VI. The Process of Restoration

Restoration does not happen overnight. It is a divine process, a sacred journey that God orchestrates over time, shaped by His wisdom, timing, and grace. Just as a master artist takes time to repair a damaged masterpiece, God patiently and lovingly restores our hearts, our purpose, and our identity. But, we must be willing participants in this divine process. Whether our hearts have been broken by grief, betrayal, failure, or disillusionment, the road back to wholeness takes time, requiring surrender, faith, and perseverance. Restoration is about discovering strength through surrender, finding hope in hardship, and trusting God with the most broken parts of our story.

In this section, we will explore three vital truths about the process of restoration: how it unfolds as a journey, the importance of trusting God's timing, and the necessity of surrendering to His loving hands as He rebuilds and reshapes our lives.

> *"And the God of all grace... after that ye have suffered a while, make you perfect, stablish, strengthen, settle you"*
> I Peter 5:10

A. *Restoration is a Journey*

One of the greatest misconceptions about restoration is that it happens instantly. In reality, restoration is a step-by-step journey that often involves healing, unlearning, relearning, and trusting again. It takes time for a wounded heart to mend, for broken trust to be rebuilt, and for clarity to return after a season of confusion.

Think of the life of Job. He lost everything -his children, his health, his wealth. Yet, in the end, God restored him. But, Job's restoration was not immediate. He wrestled with grief, doubt, and questions.

> Job 23:10
> *"But he knoweth the way that I take: when he hath tried me, I shall come forth as gold."*

He had to walk through the valley of suffering before he saw the light of renewal. Job's situation reminds us that God is not absent in the process. He is very much present and is refining us through it. Restoration also requires our participation. Like the Israelites wandering in the wilderness, sometimes we must let go of old mindsets before we can walk into a promised future. That transformation, internal and external, can only happen in God's timing and through God's ways. Remember, God said His thoughts are not our thoughts and our ways are not His ways (Isaiah 55:8). We must not lean or depend on our own understanding, but in all our ways we must acknowledge Him (Proverbs 3:5).

B. *Trusting in God's Perfect Timing for Restoration*

We live in a world of instant gratification. However, God operates on an eternal timeline. What seems delayed to us is often perfectly scheduled in God's divine plan. The hardest part of any restoration is often the waiting, when the pain still lingers and the promise has not yet been fulfilled. And, our restoration can be seemingly delayed, but as Romans 8:28 says, *"And we know that all things work together for good to them that love God, to them who are the called according to his purpose."* We must patiently wait for all parts to come together.

Abraham waited twenty-five years for Isaac from the time he was told he would become the father of a great nation. Joseph waited over a decade for deliverance from prison. David waited years to become king after being anointed. Even Jesus waited thirty years before beginning His public ministry. Ecclesiastes 3:11 says, *"He hath made every thing beautiful in his time."* Not in our time but in *His*. We may not always understand the delays. But faith trusts that God sees and knows the complete picture.

C. *Allowing God to Rebuild and Reshape Your Life*

When we think of restoration, we often long for things to be as they were. But God's idea of restoration is rarely about returning to the past. In many instances, it is about moving us into something better. The process of being rebuilt often involves change, discomfort, and surrender. But, on the other side of that surrender is purpose, strength, and beauty we never imagined.

Isaiah 61:3 speaks of God giving His people *"beauty for ashes, the oil of joy for mourning, the garment of praise for the spirit of heaviness..."* God does not just clean us up. He transforms us. He builds something new from the ruins.

Nehemiah's story is a powerful example. When he heard that the walls of Jerusalem were broken down, he wept, fasted, and prayed. Then, he led the charge to rebuild. The process was marked by opposition, fatigue, and fear, but the people trusted God, and the wall was rebuilt in just fifty-two days (Nehemiah 6:15). What looked impossible became reality through obedience and surrender.

Similarly, in our own lives, rebuilding may mean changing habits, releasing bitterness, embracing community, or stepping into unfamiliar territory. It means allowing God to remove what is broken and replace it with His truth and design for our life.

> *"And be not conformed to this world: but be ye transformed by the renewing of your mind..."*
> Romans 12:2

Romans 12:2 urges us, *"And be not conformed to this world: but be ye transformed by the renewing of your mind..."* Transformation begins in the mind, and restoration flows from renewed thinking rooted in God's Word, not the ways of the world.

The process of restoration is not always easy, but it is always sacred. When we commit to the journey, trust God's timing, and yield to His rebuilding hand, we step into a life more whole, more purposeful, and more aligned with His will. God never wastes our pain. Rather, He uses it to write stories of redemption, healing, and hope. And as we are restored, we become vessels through which others can find the courage to begin their own restoration journeys. Let God complete the work He began in you - one faithful step at a time.

VII. How to Receive Restoration

Restoration is a gift, and like any gift, it must be received. God is always willing and able to restore what has been lost, broken, or worn down in our lives, but we must posture ourselves to receive His healing work. Just as fertile soil is needed for a seed to take root and grow, our hearts must be open, willing, and surrendered for restoration to begin.

This section explores how to receive restoration by opening our hearts to God, embracing the roles of repentance and forgiveness (as needed), and learning to walk in patient hope as the process unfolds. Restoration is not a passive experience. It is a sacred collaboration between the loving hands of the Father and the surrendered heart of His child: you.

A. *How to Open Your Heart to God's Restoration*

Opening your heart to God's restoration begins with honesty, the kind of raw honesty that admits, "I'm not okay, and I need help." Many people carry hidden pain, disappointments, and failures behind smiles or by keeping busy. Yet, God is not intimidated or deterred by our wounds. He invites us to bring our full selves before Him, not the masked version, but the authentic, unadulterated one.

David was called a man after God's own heart not because he was flawless, but because he was open. He poured out his soul before God with brutal honesty. In Psalm 51:17, David declares, *"The sacrifices of God are a broken spirit: a broken and a contrite heart, O God, thou wilt not despise."* This is the posture that welcomes restoration.

> *"The sacrifices of God are a broken spirit: a broken and a contrite heart, O God, thou wilt not despise."*
> Psalm 51:17

To open your heart is to invite God into the rooms you have closed off, places of old grief, unanswered prayers, shame, regret, or betrayal. You may be afraid of what He will find there, but know this: God already sees it. He just wants your permission to begin the healing process.

This process often starts with a quiet decision. Maybe, it is the act of dusting off your Bible, whispering a prayer through tears, or writing a letter to God expressing to the best of your ability everything you feel inside. It might be seeking out a mentor, counselor, or pastor. Each step cracks the door a little wider for God's grace to flood in. Please note- Do not make the mistake of believing you must fix yourself before going to God. Go broken. Go empty. He specializes in restoration, not perfection.

B. *The Role of Repentance, Forgiveness, and Reconciliation*

Restoration is deeply tied to the healing of our relationships with God, with others, and with ourselves. This often begins with repentance, a spiritual turning point where we acknowledge where we have gone astray and realign our hearts with God's will. Repentance is not about shame; it is about returning. Acts 3:19 promises, *"Repent ye therefore, and be converted, that your sins may be blotted out, when the times of refreshing shall come from the presence of the Lord."* Did you catch that? Refreshing follows repentance. When we turn back to God, we make room for His restoration to begin.

But repentance must be coupled with forgiveness. Sometimes, it is forgiving ourselves for our past. Other times, it is letting go of resentment toward others who have wounded us. This is rarely easy. But unforgiveness is like poison in the soul. It prevents healing and keeps us trapped in yesterday's pain. That is exactly where Satan wants us to reside.

Jesus makes it clear: *"For if ye forgive men their trespasses, your heavenly Father will also forgive you"* (Matthew 6:14).

> *"For if ye forgive men their trespasses, your heavenly Father will also forgive you"*
> Matthew 6:14

Forgiveness does not mean the hurt did not matter; it means you are choosing to release its hold over you. You are releasing that burden to God.

Reconciliation, when possible, is the fruit of this inner work. It is the restoration of peace where there was once conflict. But even when full reconciliation with a person is not safe or possible, you can reconcile within by coming to terms with your past, releasing bitterness, and choosing to walk forward with grace. While restoration does not erase the past, it rewrites your relationship with it, giving you a healthier perspective. Through repentance and forgiveness, you reclaim your peace and dignity. This allows you to walk with your head lifted rather than hanging in shame or depression.

C. *Embracing Patience and Hope During the Process of Restoration*

Restoration is rarely immediate. It unfolds like the slow blooming of a flower, layer by layer, over time. This can be frustrating when we are desperate for relief or eager to move on. But in God's timing, the process matters as much as the outcome. He uses time to shape us, stretch us, and root us more deeply in His love.

Romans 5:3-5 says, *"We glory in tribulations also: knowing that tribulation worketh patience; and patience, experience; and experience, hope: and hope maketh not ashamed..."* This verse reveals that patience is not passive. It is a spiritual muscle developed through endurance, leading to a hope that does not disappoint.

When you are in the middle of your restoration journey, it can feel like nothing is changing. But trust this: God is working behind the scenes. Just as a seed sprouts roots before it ever breaks the surface of the soil, God is doing unseen work in your life that will bear fruit in due time.

Waiting seasons are sacred. They teach us to trust God, not just for the outcome, but for His companionship along the way. He is not just the Restorer; He is also the Shepherd who walks with us through the valleys (Psalm 23:4). During this time, it is essential to speak life over yourself. Stay in the Word. Surround yourself with community. Write down what God is doing, even in small ways. Celebrate progress. Let gratitude be your companion. Be careful to not attempt to rush what God is doing in you. The deeper the needed healing, the longer the work may take, and the stronger the foundation will be for the life He is building.

VIII. Living in the Fullness of Restoration

Many people experience God's healing touch but do not know how to walk in the "after." They struggle to sustain their restored relationships, dreams, or sense of identity. Yet, God's heart is not only to redeem the broken places but to empower us to thrive. In this section, we will explore what it means to live in that wholeness, maintain what God has rebuilt, and take our restoration one step further by helping others find theirs.

A. *How to Walk in the Fullness of What God Has Restored*

To walk in fullness is to walk with intention. It means embracing who you are now in Christ, not defined by your past pain, but by God's promises. In II Corinthians 5:17, Paul writes, *"Therefore if any man be in Christ, he is a new creature: old things are passed away; behold, all things are become new."* This newness is not just symbolic; it is also transformative.

After being restored, it is crucial to align your thoughts, actions, and identity with what God says is now true of you. That may mean breaking old habits of thinking, releasing shame, or setting new boundaries that reflect your healed state. It is easy to slip back into fear, insecurity, or self-sabotage, but fullness requires faith-filled living.

Begin each day by reaffirming your new identity in Christ. Speak life over your day. Remind yourself: *I am not who I used to be. I am restored, renewed, and walking in the grace of God.* Let your decisions reflect that reality, from how you treat others to what you think about yourself.

Walking in fullness means walking in freedom, not fear. It also means trusting God to reveal new purpose. Restoration is not the end. Rather, it is the launching point for the next chapter of your calling.

> *"Therefore if any man be in Christ, he is a new creature: old things are passed away; behold, all things are become new."*
> II Corinthians 5:17

B. *Maintaining Restored Health, Relationships, and Dreams*

God's restoration is powerful, but it must be tended. Like a garden, it needs care and protection to flourish long-term. That means continuing to invest in the areas God has restored: your emotional health, your relationships, your dreams, and your spiritual walk.

Proverbs 4:23 reminds us, *"Keep thy heart with all diligence; for out of it are the issues of life."* Guarding your heart is part of maintaining your restoration. Avoid the environments, conversations, or behaviors that once led to harm. Instead, stay rooted in God's Word, surrounded by healthy community, and guided by wise counsel.

Restored relationships also require humility and maintenance. Communicate honestly. Practice forgiveness regularly. Do not expect perfection, but do expect growth. When conflicts arise, do not retreat into old patterns. Choose grace, remembering how far God has brought you.

Your dreams, too, must be nurtured. Maybe God revived a passion that once lay dormant. Now, it is your job to take steps of faith whether small or bold. Keep dreaming with God. Keep moving forward, even when progress is slow.

> *"Keep thy heart with all diligence; for out of it are the issues of life."*
> Proverbs 4:23

Remember, maintenance is not about fear of loss. It is about honoring what God has done. Like Nehemiah, who rebuilt Jerusalem's walls and then stationed guards to protect them (Nehemiah 7:1), you must safeguard your restoration with wisdom and prayer. Do not allow others or yourself to tear down what God has craftily formed.

C. *The Responsibility of Helping Others Experience Restoration*

Once you have experienced God's restoration, you carry something powerful: a testimony. Your healing, your freedom, your transformation is not just for you. It is meant to be shared. Revelation 12:11 says, *"And they overcame him by the blood of the Lamb, and by the word of their testimony..."* Your story has overcoming power.

There are people in your life right now who are waiting for someone to show them that restoration is possible. They may feel lost in shame or convinced their situation is beyond repair. But when they hear your story -when they see the change in you- it can ignite hope.

Helping others does not always mean preaching. Sometimes, it is about being present. Listening. Praying with someone. Sharing a Bible verse that once held you together. Or simply saying, "I've been where you are, and I know God can bring you out."

Furthermore, you do not need to have all the answers. Just be willing to share your testimony. Be a living example of what God can do. Be bold in love and generous with encouragement. Whether through mentoring, serving, or simply living authentically, you become a vessel of restoration to others. Remember, God is no respecter of persons (Romans 2:11; Acts 10:34). What He does for one, He can do for others.

If you desire God's restorative power in your life, pray this prayer.

Gracious Father,
You are the God who restores what is broken, the One who brings beauty from ashes and hope from despair. Today, I come before you with an open heart, acknowledging the places in my

life that are dry, damaged, or lost. I lay down the pieces, every shattered dream, every wounded part of my story, and I trust you to redeem them with Your loving hands.

Lord, restore my soul. Where I've grown weary, breathe new life. Where I've strayed, lead me back to your path. Heal the wounds I cannot reach, and renew the joy I thought was gone forever.

Restore relationships that have been broken by pain, silence, or misunderstanding. Revive purpose where I've felt aimless. Rebuild the ruins of my faith where doubt has crept in. And restore in me a steadfast spirit, a heart that trusts, worships, and follows You no matter what.

I believe, Lord, that nothing is beyond Your power to restore. So, I wait with hope, knowing that Your timing is perfect and Your love is unending. Thank You for being the Restorer of all things. I place my life, my story, and my future in Your hands.

In Jesus' name,
Amen

He Restores

When all was lost, and hope grew dim,
When every song became a hymn
Of sorrow sung in silent pain
He whispered, "Child, I'll make you whole again."
The dreams I buried deep in dust,
The broken vows, the shattered trust,
The years I thought were gone for good
He gathered all and understood.
With tender hands, not filled with wrath,
He cleared debris from sorrow's path.
And in the ruins of my despair,
He built a throne of mercy there.
He did not shame me for my fall,
Nor scorn the tears I dared recall.
Instead, He knelt beside my ache
And breathed new life into my wake.
He mended wounds I never voiced,
And gave me beauty for my choice
To come to Him with all my mess
And trust His heart to heal, to bless.
Now morning breaks where night once lay,
And mercy meets me every day.
The ashes speak, "He makes things new!"
And every scar now points to truth.
Restored, not just to what was before
But greater still to achieve so much more.
For in His hands, the broken rise
And see the world through healed eyes.
So let the weary take heart, too
He's not just willing, but faithful and true.
What's torn, what's lost, what seems too far
He restores us, if we come just as we are.

Dr. C.

NOTES

NOTES

NOTES

NOTES

NOTES

Conclusion: Stepping into the New

As you come to the close of this book, know this: your journey is not ending. It is just beginning. You have walked through pages filled with truth, testimony, and teaching about breakthrough, healing, and restoration. And if your heart has been stirred, it is because God is inviting you into a deeper encounter with Him. What you have read is not merely information. It is a divine invitation.

Breakthrough is not a concept reserved for the few. It is the birthright of every believer who dares to believe God is still active, still powerful, and still faithful. Healing is not limited to physical restoration. It is the mending of hearts, the clearing of minds, and the renewal of identity. And restoration is not just about getting back what was lost. It is about becoming all you were created to be, through the love and power of a redeeming God.

Perhaps, you read this book during a season of great pain, confusion, or waiting. Maybe you have felt stuck, forgotten, or worn thin by life's battles. If so, hear this clearly: **God has not forgotten you.** He *sees* you. He knows every detail of your journey, and He specializes in bringing purpose out of pain.

This is your season. Not because circumstances are perfect, but because God is present. The same God who parted the Red Sea, who raised the dead, who restored the broken is the same God who is working in your life right now. There is nothing too far gone He cannot redeem. No wound too deep He cannot heal. No chain too strong He cannot break.

So, what now?

Now, you walk forward. You pray with expectation. You live with renewed hope. You declare God's promises over your life even before they come to pass. You speak life where there has been death. You forgive where there has been bitterness. You pursue God with all your heart, knowing He is the author and finisher of your story.

Let the testimonies in this book fuel your faith. Let the prayers become your own. Let the Scriptures be your foundation. And let your life become a living example of what it means to experience breakthrough, walk in healing, and live in full restoration.

Do not look back. Do not settle. This is not just a chapter in your life; it is a divine turning point. What the enemy meant for harm, God is turning for good. What was broken, God is making whole. What was delayed, God is now releasing in His perfect time.

Your season has come.

Step into it, with courage, with faith, and with eyes fixed on the one who makes all things new.

Additional Books by the Author

Pub. Speaking in the Spir. (2002)
Do You Know God? (2004)
Unleashed Anger (2005)
Unleashed Anger Daily Prayer (2005)
Two of a Kind (2006)
Dare to Succeed by Breaking Through Barriers (2007)
Dare to Succeed Prayer Guide (2007)
Through the Storm (2007)
Lord, Teach Me to...Blessing! (2007)
The Preacher's Daughter (2007)
The Preacher's Son (2009)
Where is Your Joppa? (2009)
From Despair, through Determination, to Victory! (2009)
Fear Not (2011)
Mayhem in the Hamptons (2012)
After the Dust Settles (2013)
A Mother's Heart (2013)
A Diamond in the Rough (2013)
The Power of a Woman (2013)
365 Days of Encouragement (2013)
A Touch in the Dark (2014)
Broken Chains (2014)
I Have Fallen (2014)
The Bottom Line (2015)
Set Free (2015)
Daughter, God Loves You (2016)
A Mother's Heart II (2016)
Living a Balanced Life (2016)
Kimara & Aaron...Disneyland (2016)
Embracing Womanhood (2017)
A Mother's Heart III (2017)
Web of Lies (2017)
Time is Running Out (2017)
Revisiting Grammar & Business Writing Essentials (2017)
Test Preparation: Writing Essentials, Mathematics Review & Reasoning Skills (2017)
The Making of Dr. C. (2018)
Claim Your Inheritance (2018)
Women's Study Bible New International Version (2018)
Christian Inspiration (2019-2023)
Safety in Him (2019)
A Mother's Heart IV (2019)

A is for Adam (2019)
Have You Walked in My Shoes? (2019)
Prepare for Battle (2019)
B is for Babel (2020)
C is for Christ (2020)
D is for David (2020)
E is Eve (2020)
F is for Forgiveness (2020)
G is for Givers (2020)
H is for Helping Others (2020)
I is for Idols (2020)
J is for Joseph (2020)
K is for Kindness (2020)
The Last Shall Be First: An Analysis of the Systemic Subdivide of Black America (2021)
L is for Love (2021)
M is for Mary (2021)
N is for Noah's Ark (2021)
is for Obedience (2021)
Rest in Him: Scriptures for Daily Peace (2021)
P is for Paul the Apostle (2021)
Q is for Queen Esther (2021)
Be Ye Inspired Vol. 1 (2021)
R is for Ruth (2021)
Be Ye Inspired Vol. II (2022)
S is for Samuel (2022)
T is for Truth (2022)
U is for Unconditional Love (2022)
V is for Victory (2022)
W is for Worship (2022)
X is for Xerxes (2022)
Y is for You (2022)
Pearls of Wisdom (2022)
Z is for Zachariah (2022)
Pearls of Wisdom Quotes & Journal (2022)
Shift Your Narrative (2023)
Living Life Without a Mask: Authentically & Unapologetically You (2023)
Dismantling System Racism and Its Effects (2024)
Naked Before God (2024)

About the Author

Dr. Cassundra White-Elliott is a dynamic and multi-faceted individual, excelling in various roles as an educator, English professor, author, publisher, and pastor. With a strong foundation in education, literature, and faith-based leadership, Dr. White-Elliott has dedicated her career to fostering growth, empowerment, spiritual awareness, and social change.

Starting her academic journey with a Bachelor of Arts in Education, Dr. White-Elliott laid the groundwork for her passion for teaching and learning. She recognized the power of education as a tool for transformation and dedicated herself to empowering students to reach their full potential.

Building upon her undergraduate studies, Dr. White-Elliott pursued a Master of Arts in English Composition, delving deep into the intricacies of writer's agency and voice. Armed with a keen understanding of the written word, she honed her skills as a writer, educator, and advocate for marginalized voices in literature.

Continuing her quest for knowledge and expertise, Dr. White-Elliott earned her Ph.D. in Education, specializing in curriculum development and professional studies. Her doctoral research focused on African American English Vernacular and educational biases against its use.

As an educator, Dr. White-Elliott brings passion, creativity, and expertise to her role as an English professor. Through engaging lectures, thought-provoking discussions, and innovative teaching methods, she inspires students to explore the complexities of literature, language, and culture while fostering critical thinking and empathy.

Outside of academia, Dr. White-Elliott is a prolific author, using her writing to amplify marginalized voices and advocate for social change. Her published works span a wide range of genres, from scholarly articles and essays to faith-based and fictional novels, exploring themes of spirituality and social justice.

Driven by a desire to provide a platform for under-represented writers, Dr. White-Elliott founded a publishing company (CLF Publishing Collaborative, LLC), dedicated to promoting diverse voices and empowering authors to share their stories with the world. As the founder and CEO, she strives to challenge stereotypes, dismantle barriers, and foster understanding and empathy across diverse communities.

In addition to her academic and literary pursuits, Dr. White-Elliott is also a dedicated pastor of International Women's Commission, using her platform to guide individuals on their spiritual journeys and fostering a sense of community and belonging. With a focus on love, compassion, and individual growth, she also uses her platform to advocate for the Body of Christ to operate in the spirit of unity while fulfilling their God-given callings.

Overall, Dr. Cassundra White-Elliott's journey is a testament to the power of education, writing, and faith in driving positive change in the world. Through her dedication, passion, and unwavering commitment to changing lives, she continues to inspire others to embrace learning, celebrate diversity, and work towards a more just and equitable society.

www.ingramcontent.com/pod-product-compliance
Lightning Source LLC
Chambersburg PA
CBHW040318170426
43197CB00021B/2952